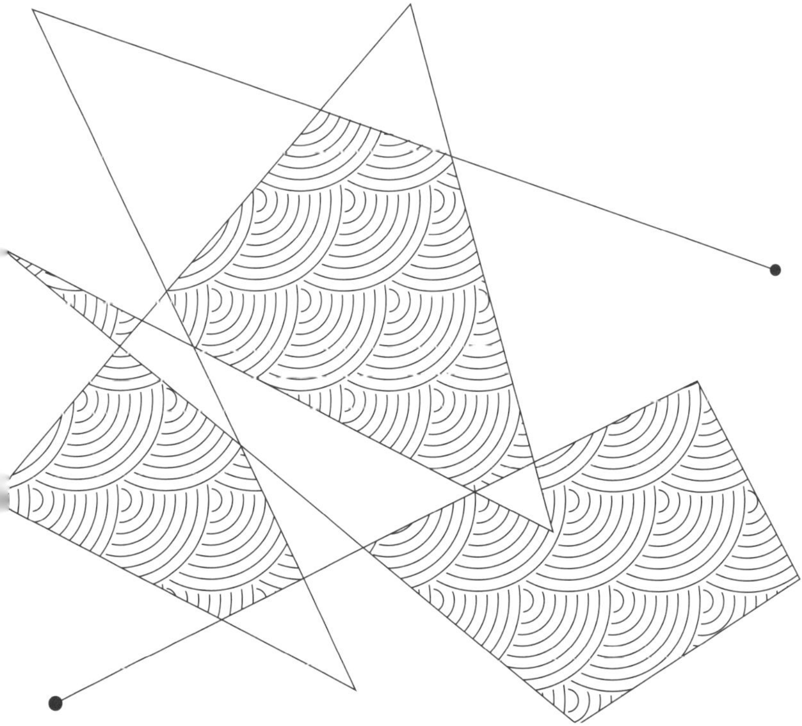

CATHARINA VAN DELDEN

CROWDSOURCED INNOVATION

REVOLUTIONIZING OPEN INNOVATION WITH CROWDSOURCING

INSIGHTS AND BEST PRACTICES FROM INNOSABI

Crowdsourced Innovation

Revolutionizing Open Innovation with Crowdsourcing

Publisher

innosabi GmbH

Catharina van Delden

Widenmayerstraße 50 | 80538 Munich | Germany

info@innosabi.com | www.innosabi.com

Graphic Design and Layout

Julia Gackstetter and Gisel·la Sapiña Febrero

ISBN: 978-3-0004-6081-4

Release date: November 2014

1st edition reprint 2016

Printed in Germany by BluePrint AG | Lindberghstraße 17 | 80939 Munich | Germany

»To all the phenomenal crowds who have never stopped supporting innosabi along the way.«

CONTENTS

Case Studies

Perspective

PREFACE

"NEW IS ALWAYS BETTER" – that is how my friends describe my curiosity for everything that I have not seen before. Buying the cereal that we always eat for breakfast when there is a new one on the shelf? Not an option for me. Our work at innosabi allows me to live and breathe that passion every day, even sharing it with thousands of people through Crowdsourced Innovation. There is nothing more motivating than seeing new ideas come to life through a transparent, inclusive, and fair discussion. As we apply these principles with our clients and interested companies every day, the time has now come to put together our concepts and experiences. We want to share them with everybody who is interested in the influence of digital tools on the products and services we use, on business models, and on the way we work together. This book shall inspire managers who ask themselves how to face the changes that emerge from the digital transformation, who want to accelerate their innovation process with Crowdsourcing techniques and who want to ensure long-term success of their companies.

For this book, we have chosen a white cover, as we want innovation managers to truly start their thought process with an open mind and a blank piece of paper or canvas for all ideas. The core of the book consists of methods and best practices that reflect concepts in business research and sociology. All of the methodologies and best practices originated in working with our clients to solve their innovation challenges. We have shaped the structure of the book in four sections in order to help you jump right to the topics you are specifically interested in:

- Visions and paradigms: uncovering academic theories that influence Crowdsourcing, Open Innovation and User Innovation and form the framework for our methods.
- Methods and best practices: unveiling the experiences from our day to day work with Crowdsourced Innovation in various industries, giving you hands-on advice on how to tackle your innovation questions together with your network.
- Case studies: describing how companies have successfully implemented Crowdsourced Innovation in the fields of product, service, and even business model development.
- Perspective: daring to take a glimpse into what might come next and how Crowdsourced Innovation can evolve with new technologies.

Customers – in B2C as well as B2B environments – expect companies to take them and their ideas seriously, on a very individual level. What used to be seemingly impossible is now becoming reality, as new methods and technologies emerge that allow the involvement of customers in innovation processes on a large and relevant scale.

Unleash the potential of innovation by becoming obsessed with engaging your customers! Don't be scared that you might fail in your Crowdsourced Innovation approach: Just by giving it a try, you have already won. With a first, initial project you can demonstrate that your company is eager to listen to new ideas and open for a new, more transparent way of doing business.

Catharina van Delden

CEO at innosabi

»Our clients are evolving from producing entities to networked organizations – with the help of their customers.«

1

THE IMPORTANCE OF CROWDSOURCING

Frank Riemensperger

Chairman of the Executive Board at Accenture GmbH

Imagine a workforce that extends beyond your employees and moves beyond the physical boundaries of your company. A workforce consisting of any user with an access to the internet; a workforce with unlimited skills and knowledge. What might sound like utopia will quickly become reality and irrevocably change the way we do business today. The evolution of the cloud as well as the increase in social media and collaboration technologies enable organizations to access vast pools of previously untapped resources all over the world and if required in real time. Resources, which lie outside traditional organizational structures and conventional boundaries.

Channeling this potential into business objectives and aligning these new opportunities with existing processes or strategies can be challenging but once mastered, the benefits are manifold. Access to an immense, agile workforce with special insights, skills, and knowledge is key to solve some of the greatest challenges in today's organizations. With the increasing pressure to rapidly deploy new technologies and products, enterprises are challenged more than ever to gain market insight, speed up innovation, and access highly specialized skills that are often difficult to find. All these challenges can effectively be addressed by opening up your organization to external knowledge with or via Crowdsourcing solutions. And the icing on the cake is that this outside knowledge is often inexpensive or even offered for free and accessible in a timely manner. All companies will face this disruptive environment eventually, so why not embrace it today and get ahead of competition?

Although some companies are already experiencing the benefits of digitally enabled forums such as innovation exchanges and Crowdsourcing platforms, the majority of executives have not yet fully grasped the entire scope of this development with all its implications. Integrating Crowdsourcing as a strategic element in an organization can create pools of top talents gathered in virtual communities coalesced around specific business problems. This extended workforce does not only offer new and previously unavailable expertise, but also improved scaling. It can be leveraged to solve problems that may be too large, too expensive or simply too time consuming to take on exclusively internally.

There is no shortage of people willing to participate in online experiments, contests, or challenges. Individuals are surprisingly ready to work for little or no money if they get other rewards: whether it is prizes, recognition, fame, or the sense of accomplishment, they appreciate inclusion and pride in creating something new. Harnessing the energy and enthusiasm of a virtual external workforce will become crucial for companies that want to absorb and utilize this potential. The only viable way to do this successfully is to understand the crowd and its underlying motivation, which differs greatly from an employee's motivation. Of course, the current internal workforce will not become obsolete, because not every problem is suited for Crowdsourced solutions. However, it will be no longer enough to solely rely on in-house personnel to drive market research, innovation, and product development. Digital technology has brought a strong voice to those functions and is now pushing and extending the boundaries that previously defined the internal workforce. Platforms that create virtual places for an idea exchange, user and customer interaction, as well as consumer investment are transforming the brick and mortar walls around companies into porous membranes. Salaried employees and the extended virtual workforce are meeting on a level playing field in a cooperative space. The nature of work itself is changing and business leaders require new perspectives.

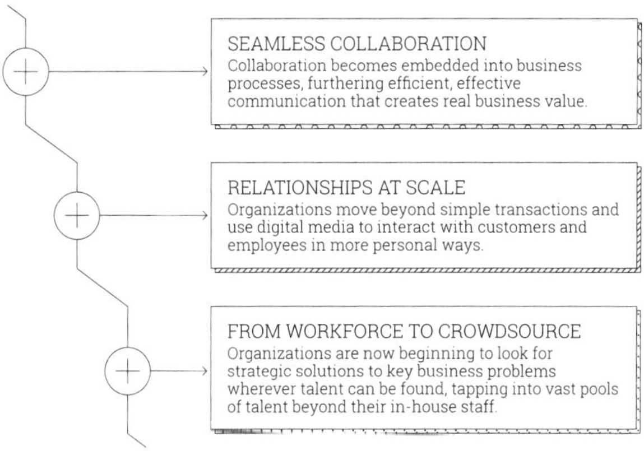

The three drivers for the growing importance and potential of Crowdsourced Innovation (based on: Accenture, 2004[i])

Market disruptors such as Facebook and innovative corporations like Adidas and General Electric are currently using Crowdsourcing techniques to solve some of their most complex problems – and everyone is taking notice. Key decision makers are wondering whether they are missing out by not connecting to this extended workforce, everywhere and in all directions. The short answer is "Yes". Predictions of leading industry analysts show that Crowdsourced Innovation is here to stay. Gartner[1] forecasts that more than half of all consumer goods manufacturers will rely on Crowdsourcing in consumer relevant innovation and R&D activities by 2017. Even more important: companies using Crowdsourcing in product development will enjoy a significant revenue multiple over their competitors by 2015. So it is time to take action now. Successful companies can no longer stay on the sideline, watching and waiting to see what will happen next. Companies need to experiment, discover, and create the next big idea instead of hoping to catch up later on.

This is especially true from an innovation management perspective. Innovation is now on top of any C-suite agenda in every organization. However, operational execution remains difficult due to the nature of innovation. The success of new products, services, and business models is uncertain and unpredictable. This makes it often hard toscale and ramp up. Yet, innovation is happening organically everywhere, whether business leaders are aware of it or not. Accessing and capturing these organically evolving innovations outside of companies' boundaries is the solution to stagnant internal innovation processes. Fortunately, communities of shared interest are forming around almost every imaginable product or idea. These communities offer the aggregated knowledge of their members and are breeding grounds for creative ideas. Often these insights can be turned into real innovations and products augmented with the existing in-house technical expertise, production capabilities, and resources. Combining external know-how with existing in-house knowledge is the key to innovation.

Jessi Hempel

Senior Writer at WIRED

»When Jeff Howe coined the term Crowdsourcing in WIRED in 2006, he set the foundation for a transformation in the way businesses interact with their consumers: crowds can reinvent customer experiences, create new innovations, or even become an essential part of a company's business model.«

2

SOMETIMES MORE IS BETTER

INTRODUCTION TO CROWDSOURCED INNOVATION

Crowdsourcing and Open Innovation had already been around for a while when we founded innosabi. The terms were appearing on management agendas and enthusiastic advocates were proclaiming it as the next big thing in business. However, we quickly realized that in most cases the concepts remained little more than buzzwords. Being closely associated with the entrepreneurial spirit and dynamic of start-ups, many companies used these methods to convey a progressive image. The actual implementations were disappointing and left much to be desired. Being convinced of the potential of Crowdsourcing and Open Innovation, we tried to determine why this was happening. We always came back to two simple reasons. First, companies failed to give the projects a proper purpose and strategic importance. Instead, Crowdsourcing and Open Innovation were mostly insignificant additions to existing structures or processes without beeing properly embedded in them. Second, without Crowdsourcing an Open Innovation strategy will not reach its full potential. The power lies in their combination. This became and still is our vision – an approach we termed Crowdsourced Innovation.

We want to help companies to start working with the crowd as an innovation partner in order to answer organizations' most important innovation and research questions. Active engagement with external parties enables constant innovation, one of the most important drivers of sustainable success and competitive advantage.

Seeking knowledge, ideas, and collaboration outside of corporate boundaries typically happens in loose and decentralized networks, connected through web technology. By giving these loose flows of information a strategic framework and connecting Crowdsourcing and Open Innovation, companies can increase the rate of success for their new products, services and even business models as they begin to focus on user needs early on and devote their development capacities to those research projects which are most promising.

Open Source Principles Outside of Software

Jeff Howe analyzed the dynamics of Crowdsourcing as a way of collaboration. His article "The rise of Crowdsourcing"[2] in the magazine WIRED defined the term combining the words "crowd" and "outsourcing". It is the process of obtaining services, ideas, or content from a large group of people rather than from internal resources like employees or suppliers – typically over the internet. To put it simply, it is the application of principles known from Open Source software development to other fields and sectors.[3] With technologies for collaboration and social networking becoming much more sophisticated, exposing problems to a widely diverse crowd of individuals and engaging their skills, experience or perspectives has become much more accessible.

We asked ourselves how Crowdsourcing can lead to innovation. Is there Crowdsourced Innovation? Answering this question requires an understanding of different concepts, some of them supported by in depth research. Open Innovation, Crowdsourcing, Swarm Intelligence as well as User Innovation come into play in order to drive innovation. The common element in all of them is a community as the central success factor. There are three main lines of thought we would like to address in more detail:

- SOURCING FROM THE CROWD: being able to tap into a large pool of resources anytime; relationships are established on a one to one basis.
- CONNECTING THE CROWD: establishing connections between the different actors in a crowd; relationships are established on a one to many basis.
- CROWDSOURCED INNOVATION: by providing access to a large pool of resources and establishing relationships amongst individuals, intelligent processes enable the creation of new knowledge and solutions.

Sourcing from the Crowd

Crowdsourced Innovation only happens when it is possible to tap into a relevant crowd; a group of individuals who possess knowledge, skills, or resources required for the innovation process. Several successful companies with often disruptive business models have already evolved around the concept of reaching relevant crowds. Examples are platforms connecting travelers with couches, beds, or futons in private homes or connecting people wanting to go from A to B with private drivers of cars rather than taxis. These business models thrive from the availability of resources from the crowd – like beds or cars – yet always establish a one to one relationship between the different actors.

Labor and knowledge can also be sourced from the crowd: micro tasks in the form of basic routines like checking content on maps or images are often distributed via the web to be completed by the general public. Examples are Amazon's Mechanical Turk, Clickworker or Gigwalk. The objective of companies employing the crowd is to get cost effective and quick access to sometimes scarce skills and knowledge anywhere, any time as needed. Platforms take fees to connect supply and demand. Even funding can be sourced from the crowd: crowdfunding companies like Kickstarter, indiegogo or Bergfürst access the crowd to get funding for companies or non-profit projects such as creating art or music. Crowdfunding raises small amounts of money from a large number of people instead of taking on board few single investors.

Connecting the Crowd

Connecting the crowd – and going beyond merely sourcing from the crowd – has triggered a social revolution. Social media has used this mechanism to connect users, who have personal relationships or similar interests and are willing to share their experiences. These communities foster constant dialogue, not necessarily pursuing a common goal or task – the connection and communication between individuals and networks creates value in itself. We have seen that the healthiest networks with high rates of communication and interaction are often those that connect a diverse set of experience, knowledge, and skills.

Sourcing from the Crowd and Connecting the Crowd

Combining the two concepts quickly brings us into the world of complex problem solving: sophisticated questions, where the crowd contributes as a team and each individual performs his or her own task, are often solved successfully by the crowd. Even though these activities can be similar, their interrelatedness and the connections between the individuals create swarm intelligence, which can eventually evolve into "the wisdom of the crowds".

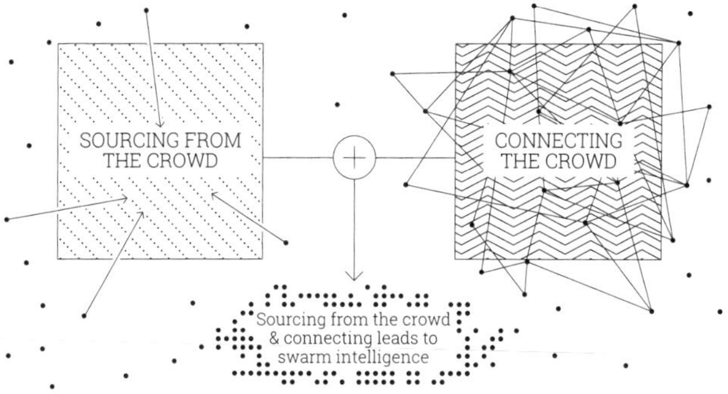

With the right processes in place, crowds can enrich Open Innovation by acting as an intelligent entity, not just a loose group of individuals.

In order to understand swarm intelligence, we can learn a lot from behavioral science or biology. Peter Miller[4] described principles that make a system smart. For example, in an ant colony no one is in charge. The system has to organize itself. This can only work if there are strong communication mechanisms and social interaction. Even though no individual ant sees the big picture, the colony can function as one cohesive entity through the contributions of the individual elements. We apply this idea of swarm intelligence in our approach. Establishing communication and social interaction among a large number of participants is the key to solve problems and generate ideas which the individual person cannot accomplish on his or her own.

Revolutionizing Open Innovation with Crowdsourcing

Traditionally internal R&D departments using insights from sales and marketing have dominated the development of innovative products, services or business models. In most cases, companies do this in isolation, behind closed doors – closed innovation, as it is called. In contrast to this, Open Innovation techniques – first described by Henry Chesbrough[5] – have been developed to access skills and knowledge outside the boundaries of a company. It helps companies to involve external parties such as end-users, prospective customers, or experts in the innovation process in order to help organizations understand needs and wishes as well as to identify new ideas and technologies. Value is created from collaborative idea generation and innovation mechanisms leading to new products, services, or even business models. Successful innovation processes, however, should not solely rely on idea generation from external sources. Internally and externally developed ideas should complement each other. The role of internal R&D is not questioned, however, it has to adapt to this new paradigm in order to unleash its full potential.

Opening innovation processes to increase the success of innovation activities have long been employed in companies, very often in the form of workshops or other offline activities. Today however, it has never been easier to reach thousands of interested and motivated

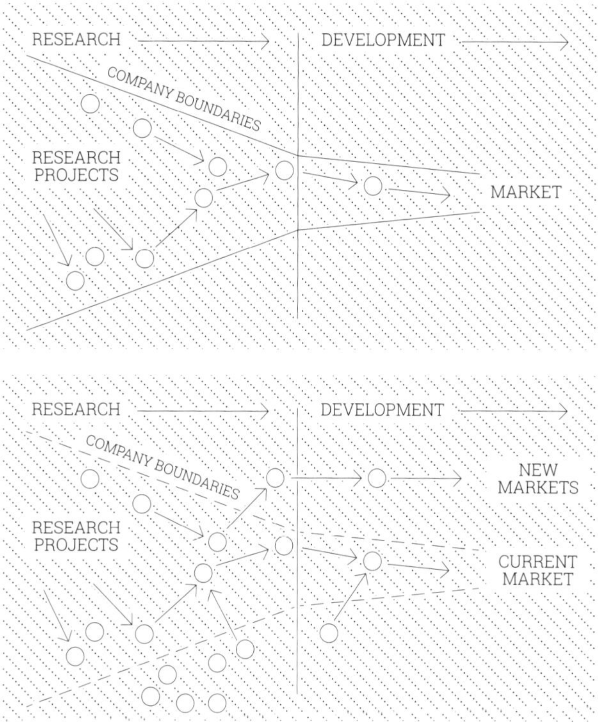

Open Innovation is enabled by permeable boundaries, allowing the exchange of information with external parties along the entire R&D process. (based on: Chesbrough, 2013[ii])

individuals for meaningful collaboration. Crowdsourcing with all its aspects supercharges and revolutionizes Open Innovation approaches, utilizing the potential of the web. We call this CROWDSOURCED INNOVATION.

With this approach, we have successfully extended the concept of Open Innovation by deliberately engaging a large pool of qualified and diverse participants. Crowdsourcing technologies combined with the power of communities significantly enhance the scale and speed of Open Innovation processes.

The advantages of Crowdsourced Innovation result primarily from three different sources:

- The research efforts focus on user needs and ideas, leading to products with a higher chance of acceptance at market entry generating the desired return on invest.
- At the same time, companies can identify promising research projects early on and allocate their resources accordingly or cut down their costs by not spending money on potentially unsuccessful research efforts.
- Above all, it builds strong and lasting customer relationships. Opening innovation processes to large teams signals transparency and makes a brand tangible and accessible – thus credible. If a customer has helped to create a new product or service, it somewhat becomes "his" or "hers". A product suddenly has a joint history with the customer leading to an emotional connection and enthusiastic word of mouth communication.

Changing consumer behavior asks for direct involvement and higher transparency: Crowdsourced Innovation provides just that. This is why Crowdsourced Innovation should be an essential part of the corporate innovation tool kit for securing opportunities for successful new products, services and business models.

Domenica Kirchmeyer

Senior Specialist Product Development at 3M

»Innovation has always been at the center of 3M's core values. But we know, that great ideas emerge from collaboration, rarely from single sparks of genius: this is why we use Crowdsourced Innovation approaches to identify new markets, untapped needs, and new ways of thinking about our innovation questions.«

3

THE EVOLUTION OF CONSUMER BEHAVIOR

When we developed the concept of Crowdsourced Innovation, our goal was to provide an answer for a critical problem that producers as well as consumers were – and still are – facing. From our own experiences as end-users, we knew how difficult it has become to find products or services that fully meet our expectations and needs. Even though companies were trying to offer new and innovative products, many appeared to be always one small step behind the growing expectations, leaving consumers as well as producers dissatisfied. We locate the reason for this gap in a profound change in consumer behavior. Instead of regarding this change as an issue, we saw its potential and made it a central driver for our methods that ultimately bring producers and consumers closer together. To fully grasp the potential of this approach and its enabling dynamics, it is necessary to understand the evolution of today's consumers – especially their behavior and how it differs from a traditional one.

During the 20th century, the emergence of mass production and the growing prosperity in many nations spurred the dynamics of modern consumerism. Consumers had the option to choose from a never before seen variety of brands and products, conveniently available and affordable in supermarkets or department stores. This changed the nature of shopping radically. Instead of merely buying food or other necessities, shopping became a leisure activity and consumption a means of expression. Manufacturers and brands fueled this development by pushing more and more products and services to the market, perpetuating the ever-expanding consumption of goods, commodities, and services. However, in this paradigm, the role of consumers was limited to simply accepting and consuming the products introduced by manufacturers or corporations. Considering the negative side effects of these practices – especially the ecological impact of excessive overconsumption and wasteful production – this is no longer viable. The importance of such issues has led to the rise of new forms of consumption, emphasizing sustainability and conscious consumption.

Presumer – a New Type of Consumer

As a consequence, a new type of consumer with a fundamentally different behavior and self-conception has started to become more prevalent. These consumers are no longer satisfied with the role as a passive recipient of products and services that are eventually offered on the market. Instead, they are advancing into areas that were traditionally held solely by producers. By shifting their focus towards product development cycles and processes before products actually hit the market, these new consumers are challenging the dominant position of companies and corporations resulting from market or brand leadership. This type of consumer does not want to simply choose a suitable product out of a broad variety; they want to have their ideal product or service. The logical step for them is to get involved in funding, developing, or designing the products and services they actually need or desire.

Since these consumers want to get engaged well before a launch of a product or service, the process of consumption begins significantly earlier and extends over a longer period compared to traditional consumer behavior. In light of this early engagement, the new generation of consumers is referred to as presumers[6] – a combination of the words "pre" and "consumer". These presumers are motivated by the aspiration to get the ideal product or service, to get it now and to be the first to have it. But above all, presumers want connections. They want to connect with the products and also through the products with the manufacturer and other users. When presumers engage with products before market launch, they establish a connection that goes far beyond their functional use or the act of consumption. The presumer has supported the idea generation and major steps in the development process and sometimes even granted funding. Being part of the product's evolution and getting engaged from the very beginning gives a whole new dimension to owning the final outcome.

Building Communities on a Shared Belief

This connection and attachment reaches beyond the single individual. Presumers who are engaged with a product before its market launch do so because they believe in it as a true advocate. This belief is shared by all involved individuals and sets a natural foundation for a community of connected presumers as well as a sense of belonging that goes far beyond the satisfaction of simply possessing a product. When pursuing a shared cause, this can even create larger movements of passionate and involved people. For example, the Ocean Cleanup Project[7] started in 2012 as the idea of a 19 year old student who planned to develop a method to extract the growing amount of plastic particles in the oceans around the world. By giving people the option to support the technology via crowdfunding, being an advocate for it in social media or actively take part in the development process, the project quickly raised more than $2 million. What is even more impressive than the amount contributed is the number of people who rallied behind the project and its environmental cause. After only two years, the project team consisted of almost 100 people and an international community of more than 35,000 supporters had formed. Even though the technology is still far from being implementable, the shared belief in its cause and the passionate community growing around it are driving the project onward.

The motivation of presumers to engage and participate is in strong contrast to what we have seen previously in traditional consumption patterns. Even though this is a fairly recent development, they are far from being a negligible niche phenomenon. Generation Y in particular is constantly seeking for novelty and engagement. They are likely to be early adopters and they are taking up an increasingly large and often vocal presence in the market. As such, they are natural presumers. In the course of this development, the mainstream market will eventually shift from consumers who wait until a product has been launched towards presumers who see the potential of a new product and who want to become an active part in its history even before it is ready to hit the market. There is no doubt that the new behavior is becoming the standard and companies can no longer afford to ignore the demand of consumers for early and respectful involvement.

Creating Opportunities for Companies and Presumers with Crowdsourced Innovation

What might appear like a threat or challenge for manufacturers at first, is actually a tremendous opportunity. As expectations and demands of users are getting increasingly complex, it is more and more difficult to address them with products and services that are developed by companies behind closed doors. Today, customers are looking beyond the functionality of a product. Unique design, lifestyle compatibility, or eco-friendliness are just some aspects that are expected of great products and services. Instead of hoping to offer a final product that satisfies the users' needs along these dimensions, producers can benefit from the intrinsic motivation of the presumers to engage. Through Crowdsourced Innovation, presumers can be involved in the development process early on, allowing them to create a product or service that meets their expectations. In addition to that, engaging presumers establishes lasting connections and attachment with the product, service, or brand

With new technologies and platforms for collaboration and consumer engagement, no step in the product development and innovation process remains unaffected. The growing number of crowdfunding platforms and user-initiated projects confirms the trend of presumers and the evolution of a new consumer behavior. It is clearly visible how motivated the new generation of consumers is to create their ideal products or services – not only in terms of functionality but also regarding authentic consumption experiences and meaningful connections. But above all, it shows how companies and their current product or service offerings are increasingly failing to fully meet the expectations of more demanding users. With customers acting beyond the simple consumption of goods, manufacturers have to extend their role outside the actual production and sales process. Connecting people through meaningful products and a shared cause will become a critical aspect for the success of businesses. Constantly involving and engaging users is a first step towards this new understanding of sustained innovation, customer satisfaction, and lasting brand loyalty.

Dr. Christoph Klingenberg
Senior Vice President Infrastructure Strategy and Member of the Infrastructure Executive Team at Deutsche Bahn

»Our customers expect us to cater for their needs not only at stations and in trains, but also demand a seamless online experience. Apart from mobile booking and improved internet access whilst traveling we offer realtime schedule and connection information as well as a realtime train tracking tool called DB radar.«

4

THE POWER OF USERS AS INNOVATORS

Aside from engaging consumers and adjusting to their new behavior, our vision of Crowdsourced Innovation is also based on another important aspect. We believe that companies need to understand and embrace the full innovative potential of their customers. Countless times, we have had to answer questions like "But what do our customers know about developing new products? What can they contribute without professional or technological skills?". This is symptomatic for a dated perspective, in which companies consider their research and development efforts as the sole source of new technologies and products. Fortunately, there is abundant evidence to convince skeptics of a paradigm shift, which is challenging the established notion of creating innovations.

The Traditional Perspective: Producers as Innovators

Innovations and technological advancements are critical drivers for modern economies and societies. Thus, it does not surprise that fostering such innovations and creating an innovative environment are taking up prominent positions on today's political and economic agenda. Funding research centers, strengthening ties between academia and businesses, or clustering industrial competences are typical actions taken in this context. This follows the assumption that innovations emerge from organizations or companies and eventually diffuse to the end-users. The arguments for this perspective are numerous. Above all, companies are expected to have the required resources, skills, and knowledge to develop innovative products and technologies. Especially in the light of the complexity of modern products, this seems plausible.

However, the traditional perspective of producers as innovators has one crucial shortcoming. Even though companies might have the required resources and expertise to innovate, they are bound by their profit orientation. If they fail to identify a potential market, they might choose not to pursue the development of a new product or service after all. Consequently, only innovations that offer the necessary incentives for the producer would emerge. But what about innovations that are beneficial for society but do not generate sufficient profit; or products that create entirely new markets only after they have been successfully introduced? This shortcoming becomes especially critical assuming that disruptive innovations and groundbreaking technologies in their early stages are often only attractive to small and unprofitable niche markets. Thus, relying solely on the innovative potential of organizations and their internal research can be risky; for the companies themselves, as well as for technological advancement as a whole.

Users as a Source of Innovations

Fortunately, there are many examples that show the exact opposite: surgeons inventing new tools, engineers programming their own software solutions or athletes developing specialized equipment. Even the World Wide Web was created by a single person who just wanted an easier way to transfer images and text to his colleagues. In countless cases, the source of innovative new products are not companies with their organized development and profit orientation, but instead independent users looking for a solution for their individual needs. The phenomenon of such inventions is called User Innovation, extensively researched by Eric von Hippel[8]. It locates the source of innovation not at the point of production and organizational R&D, but instead at the point of immediate use. These User Innovators are at the heart of a paradigm shift; one that changes our understanding of innovation and how it can be enabled.

Typically, User Innovators have needs that differ from the ones of mainstream users and consequently cannot find the appropriate products on the market. Given the lack of incentives for producers to invest in the development of such specific products, User Innovators often have no other choice than to come up with solutions for their individual situation by themselves. Since their goal is not to sell their invention or generate direct profits with it, the motivation of solving these problems is mainly intrinsic. Being driven by their own needs makes them highly motivated, persistent, and creative. In addition, they are not bound by profits, organizational structures, and production capabilities – allowing them to think and innovate outside the box. Considering these points, the innovative potential of end-users should not be underestimated.

A New Paradigm

Users who are facing a specific problem often have extensive knowledge and understanding of their need as well as its entire context. They know exactly what has to be solved and what they expect from a potential solution. Producers on the other hand have to make major efforts to acquire this information before even beginning the actual development process. What makes this especially complicated, is that this information is "sticky"[9]. Sticky information is bound to its context and thus difficult to transfer from one point to another or to put into use at another site other than its point of origin. In many cases, the problem is not only transferring the knowledge. Companies often do not know what to exactly look for or ask when exploring new territory. Consequently, despite considerable market research efforts, producers are often unable to connect the knowledge of the users regarding their specific needs with existing organizational, technological capabilities.

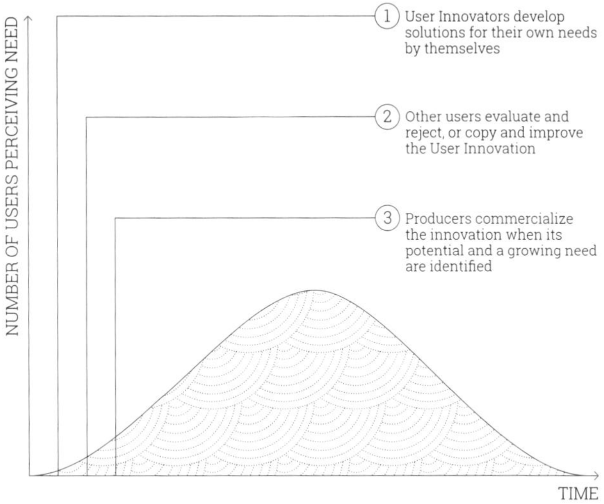

User Innovators create innovative solutions for their own needs long before companies identify the market potential and commercialize them. (based on: v. Hippel, et al., 2011[iii])

The current paradigm shift in innovation provides an answer to this issue. In this new understanding, users are not mere recipients of innovations provided by producers. Instead, they play a central and active role in the development of new products and technologies. More and more producers are embracing the innovative potential of users and start to see them as a valuable resource for innovative new products. Rather than facing the difficult task of "unsticking" the users' knowledge regarding their needs, they start to search for User Innovators and their inventions right away. Not only does this bypass the difficult identification of needs and transfer of information, it also provides the companies with the users' ideas and prototypes as a starting point for the development process.

User Innovation and User Innovators are not a rare phenomenon. Studies have shown that 5.2% of consumers in the USA[10] and 6.1% of consumers in the UK[11] engage in innovative activities, for example the modification and customization of sports equipment or tools. This amounts to a total of more than 11 million User Innovators in the USA and almost 3 million in the UK. Even more impressive than the large number of innovative individuals is the magnitude of their activities. It is estimated that the User Innovators in the UK spend close to 100,000 person-years and £3.2 billion annually on their development efforts – 1.4 times larger than the annual consumer product R&D expenditures of all firms in the UK combined.[12] Despite its scope and scale, most of this innovative potential has remained isolated at the end of the users and untapped by corporate efforts. However, more companies are beginning to recognize these User Innovators as a valuable source for the development of new products and services.

Connecting User Innovators

Of course, users have always been tinkering and inventing. In that sense, User Innovators are not a novelty, but integrating them into organizational innovation processes often is. The reason why this is easily possible to implement on a large and global scale is the internet. It is the key driver for companies to identify the relevant individuals and network with them. But above all, it has the potential to connect User Innovators with numerous like-minded people. Instead of isolated activities, innovation at the users' end can become a social process. The exchange of information and experiences allows the users to work together towards one common goal and accomplish projects that exceed the capabilities and skills of a single individual and quite possibly the ones of R&D departments. The large number of individuals with various backgrounds and skillsets is not the only factor that highlights the inherent power of User Innovators. The times when producers have exclusively held the knowledge to develop innovative products or technologies are long gone. With the enormous amounts of publicly available information on the internet, acquiring new skills is often just one mouse click away. The limiting factor is no longer one's existing expertise or the availability of expert knowledge. For User Innovators, this means that many complex problems and obstacles along the creative process are not insurmountable any more. The impact of these autodidactic opportunities will increasingly affect the potential of User Innovators, as the generation of Digital Natives makes up a larger share of our population. Already today, the initial reaction of many young adults when facing a problem is to simply "google it" and to work it out on their own.

Companies should integrate this innovative potential into their development processes and connect themselves with the relevant individuals. With the growing potential of User Innovators, this soon will become a strategic necessity and companies ignoring this trend will be outrun. To make use of the full potential that this paradigm shift brings along, companies have to systematically enable User Innovators and the communication among them. This means that the dynamic of User Innovation should be placed within an environment that encourages innovation and at the same time defines goal oriented processes and permeable boundaries to internalize and eventually commercialize the created inventions. Within such structures, a community of innovators driven by their own needs has the potential to become a valuable asset to a company's development processes. This is what eventually sets them apart from their competitors.

To create a lasting competitive advantage, organizations need to go even further than funneling User Innovations into their internal processes. There are many capable producers out there who can commercialize User Innovations. And they will look for them – if they have not already started. In order to keep the edge on this competition, it is essential to create lasting ties with these innovative users. Since User Innovators are primarily driven by a need or a problem, they could easily turn towards any organization or brand that can provide a solution or is willing to collaborate in finding one. Lasting ties cannot be established by jointly developing innovative solutions alone. An approach that integrates User Innovators into the company sustainably and for the long run also needs to foster emotional attachment and true relationships. When the user feels a personal connection to the company or to other User Innovators in the community he or she will be less likely to cooperate with other companies. The only way to get this kind of attachment is by repeatedly involving the users, pooling them in a lively community, pursuing a common goal, and sincerely appreciating their ideas. The real power of User Innovators is only starting to become visible as users continue to connect and cooperate with each other. Innovative organizations need to become an active part in this development; not just by seeing users as a source of innovation, but by sharing information, expertise, and establishing meaningful connections themselves.

Andrea Kathrin Christenson

Former Managing Director of the Doll Manufacturer Käthe Kruse

»The doll that turned into a bestseller and invigorated our company was actually based on a User Innovation: resourceful mothers had been using this technique to build dolls out of burp cloths for ages.«

5

BRANDED COMMUNITIES FOR CROWDSOURCED INNOVATION

Andreas Nicklas

Senior Executive Business Development & Social Commerce at Lithium Europe

A community brings groupings of people together through common interests. Some personal relationships might exist within groupings, but in most cases members of a community do not know each other beforehand. A single person might be a member of several different communities. In contrast personal relationships, however, are a prerequisite for social networks, and common interests can exist within social networks, but are not required. Every person has only one social network based on personal relationships.

The concepts of communities and social networks have existed for thousands of years. Today, however, the internet and its capabilities for bidirectional dialogue provides an infrastructure for communities and social networks, enabling location-independent communication. Through its asynchronous nature it is even independent of temporal restrictions. The internet's capacity for dialogue paved the way for web-based communities and social networks. The internet has become truly "social".

Branded and Non-branded Communities

A community can be something as simple as a group of people interested in cooking. Their shared interest is the preparation of food based on recipes. Chefkoch is an example for an independent, non-branded community where community members share and create recipes and experiences around cooking. Within this community, the user generated content and the user's expertise are relevant, but any personal relationship is irrelevant. Herein lies the difference between communities and social networks: the probability of finding a connoisseur of Mexican black bean dishes amongst personal Facebook friends is relatively low and a personal social network is of limited use. However, the personal social network is adequate to invite friends to a Mexican black bean dinner, whereas the Chefkoch community provides the benefits of a network of cooking connoisseurs, who are connected voluntarily without being members of a brand or institution. Such a community is a non-branded community. In contrast, branded communities are connected to a company or a particular organization. Branded or owned communities are usually hosted on a website of a company or organization. However, there are many crossovers of communities and social networks like Twitter, for example, where people can organize on topics and/or relationships.

Reach and Relevance

The key strength of social networks is building and maintaining relationships. Therefore companies operate so called fanpages in Facebook where members can become fans of a company, brand, its products, or services. The objective of these companies is to build relationships with their target groups that are active on social networks. The high number of fans, such as LIDL's 10 million[13] international fans, prove that these fanpages work well and reach many people. However, the key question to be answered is whether it is possible to not just achieve reach but engage consumers or generate customer loyalty through social networks. The answer is: unfortunately only on a very limited basis. Market statistics show that only 6% of fans[14] engage with a fanpage without any accompanying promotional activities, for example to read published corporate content. Why do those pages fail to fully engage consumers? Two important elements are missing: trusted user-generated content and relevance.

But these are exactly the elements that communities can provide. Since communities organize themselves based on interests and content, RELEVANCE is a given. Target groups visit these communities voluntarily to find content, like-minded people, help, and experts in order to obtain knowledge or discuss as well as share topics corresponding to their specific interests. If a person has questions or suggestions on a specific topic, they can communicate easily with members of a respective community.

Communities – just like social networks – create REACH. But the method differs: search engines prefer user-generated content produced in communities. When someone searches for particular information, communities with appropriate content will appear at the top of the results page. If it is a branded community, target groups who currently are not customers will potentially visit the website where the branded community is hosted. Branded communities therefore generate reach and relevance at the same time due to user generated content. This is a significant advantage over a social network like Facebook, which generates reach more or less without relevance.

The relationship between reach and relevance is crucial: reach is achieved first by addressing target groups through social channels and communities. Then the real prospects will be won with relevant content generated by communities, because members of a target group will only become a real prospect or a customer when their current and specific needs are addressed. In practice, the two different methods of generating reach with social networks and communities can be combined when social networks are integrated into communities. The community acts as a social hub and the advantages of both methods complement each other reaching the broadest coverage.

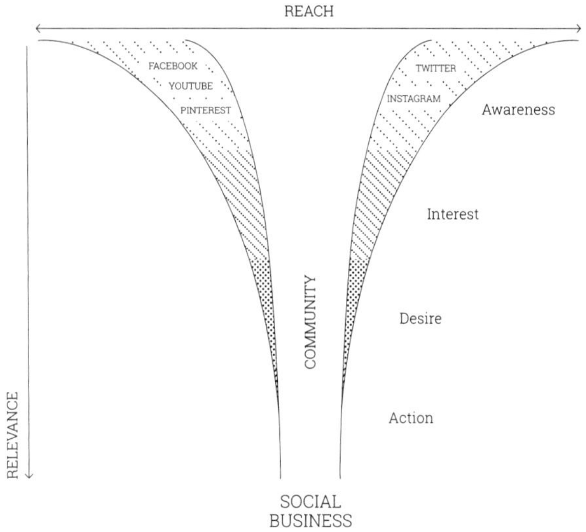

While social networks primarily create reach, communities create relevance built on user generated content supplemented with reach. (based on: Wu, 2013[iv])

Peer-to-Peer versus Traditional Channels

Before the internet has enabled social media and social business, target groups and customers were served via traditional media. These are called outbound or inbound directed channels. Examples of traditional outbound channels are print media, radio, and television, but also the internet in the form of banner ads. Call centers are an example of an inbound channel, where a customer calls to receive help, can place a service request or make a purchase. Email can serve as both an outbound and inbound channel.

Companies tend to address their audiences by carrying content unidirectionally to their target audience via traditional outbound channels: this is commonly referred to as push marketing. Social channels like Twitter, YouTube, or Facebook are often used similarly to traditional media channels for push marketing. An example is the Facebook fanpage, where content is distributed based on a 1:n model. This is known as paid media, because companies have to pay for the creation and distribution of enterprise content and advertising. Similarly, social channels are used today like traditional inbound channels for customer service (a 1:1 model) and are as a consequence perceived like traditional channels. Because social channels are used like traditional media channels, users experience "Social as just another Channel".

However, the real power of social media is the two-way communication, the dialogue: creating, distributing, discussing, and sharing knowledge as well as user-generated content are the major benefits. This n:n or peer-to-peer model consists of two-way streets where everybody can engage in bidirectional conversations: members of target groups can talk amongst themselves, they can discuss topics with companies, and companies can communicate with the target groups. This way social media becomes much more than just another channel, because it incorporates and encourages peer-to-peer communication, user-generated content, and its reciprocal involvement. User-generated content is then referred to as earned media, because it is created by the participants and not the company. Hence, the full potential of social media can only be harnessed through the peer-to-peer model. Furthermore the peer-to-peer model allows to integrate target groups into organizations enabling a shared economy which is a prerequisite for Crowdsourced Innovation.

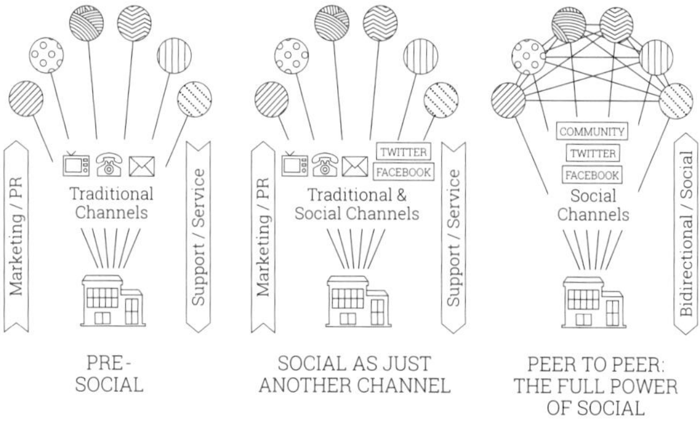

The power of social lies in its peer-to-peer model, which enables bidirectional communications and allows the integration of target groups. (based on: Wu, 2013v)

Trust Built on User Generated Content

A study published by Nielsen[15] shows that target groups can be most successfully reached through earned media. Simply because 84% of the audiences trust user generated content. Today's consumers rely on peers, friends, colleagues, or experts. This statistic illustrates a paradigm shift from push to pull marketing: target groups often trust user-generated content more and can therefore be addressed successfully through pull marketing, i.e. creating and deploying user-generated content. Consequently trust in a company's communication with target groups, or trust in a brand, product, or service is gained primarily through user-generated content. The capacity to enable peer-to-peer dialogue is a prerequisite for the creation and sharing of user-generated content. Using an internet community is the best way to achieve this.

Experiences and Transparency

Social media has helped customers gain more power in B2B and B2C marketplaces because it offers a platform for participants to share personal experiences and observe the experiences of others. It has helped to create an environment of brutal transparency. Nothing is hidden. As a consequence traditional marketing methods cannot gloss over inconvenient truths about defective products, poor services, or unpopular brands. Thus push marketing is becoming ineffective and sometimes even harmful when services or products are not completely suitable for the market. But with the help of Crowdsourced Innovation, social media provides many great opportunities for brands, products, and services to be adapted to the needs of target consumers. And if suitable products or services hit the market, transparency is turning into a key advantage resulting in viral word-of-mouth marketing.

Expertise

Target customers share not only their experiences with products but also their expertise regarding the features and application of products and services. Today's customer, whether in B2C or B2B markets, uses the internet to gather expertise. The more complex the products or services are the more intensely the internet is used for this purpose. This expertise is conveyed through content. A great place to find this kind of content is alongside a company's owned content, especially within communities next to earned content. That is because people produce and share information and knowledge within communities, and in most cases topical experts are part of these communities. The dialogue that produces expert knowledge takes place in open forums, Q&A forums, or blogs. Here user-generated content is offered in a user-friendly way with the help of knowledge bases. Internet search engines like Google will eventually prefer such user-generated content. As a consequence, target consumers are much better informed when they compare products or services, in particular before they make purchasing decisions. With this increased knowledge, these consumers become a valuable and equitable source for optimizing products and services or developing new ones through the principles of Crowdsourced Innovation.

Engagement, Enlistment, and Advocates

The content-based, two-way dialogue is the hallmark of peer-to-peer communities. Such dialogue cultivates contact and relationships with consumers and then intimately binds them to brands, products, and services. This engagement, achieved through user-generated content, shared experiences, imparted expertise, and transparency, is also generating trust. Engagement combined with a positive customer experience leads to enlistment. Enlistment occurs when a customer acts for the purposes of a business or organization: for example, when one customer during a purchase process answers the questions and service concerns of another. In the best case, the customer defends the brands, products, and services against criticism and recommends them through word-of-mouth advertising. The customer has become a company advocate. Customers or prospective customers who are advocating for a company or organization can be found in any vibrant, successful community. They are called super fans and they usually make up about 1%[16] of the total members in a community. Despite their small numbers they have significant influence; they are considered experts and are recognized and trusted within the community. They become the main influencers. Whereas engagement binds a prospect or customer to a company, enlistment integrates and activates a customer within a company resulting in shared economy. The customer is becoming a purchasing consultant, customer service provider, or even a new product developer. This is why engagement and enlistment are key success factors for Crowdsourced Innovation.

Vibrancy

We have learned that on the foundation of communities – ideally integrated with social channels and social networks – reach, relevance, trust, expertise, engagement, enlistment, and advocates can be built. The necessary basis for this work is the bidirectional dialogue and the consequential creation of user-generated content. Communities based on the peer-to-peer model provide a firm foundation for customer engagement and enlistment. However, this is only true if the communities are vibrant and dynamic. If the members of a community do not enter into dialogue with each other, then they do not generate user-content. If, for example, customers do not help other customers in a social support community, then the community is worthless. Therefore, vibrant communities and their active dialogues are key to success. Unfortunately, these key factors are often underestimated in practice, which is why 70%[17] of all communities fail. Due to missing vibrancy they provide no value and get shut down. To gain vibrancy, it is essential to incorporate elements of behavioral psychology, gamification, and social intelligence in the construction of communities and to promote appropriate and dynamic dialogue structures. However, translating these important aspects into functioning algorithms is complex and requires extensive know-how. It explains why many communities without such algorithms or the skill to develop them do not succeed.

Social Business versus Social Media

Social business is built on a variety of social business processes like social marketing, social commerce, social support, social loyalty and Crowdsourced Innovation. Typically, these social business processes are closely interconnected and cannot be considered in isolation. For example, social support requests and the possible solutions stemming from a community could contain valuable information for ideation processes to improve product characteristics and product quality.

Reviews, ratings and recommendations created by community members in the context of social commerce often include valuable information for the improvement of products or useful features that distinguish a product from a competitor's. This is why user-generated content is so valuable for Crowdsourced Innovation, especially when originating in other social business processes. And conversely, user generated content that originates in Crowdsourced Innovation can be highly valuable in social marketing or social commerce processes.

However social started with social media and in many cases social media channels like Facebook are still being used like traditional media channels. Departments like brand marketing are often responsible for these social media activities and objectives that still function in the traditional manner of advertising campaigns. But the campaign driven distribution of branded content through push marketing in social media channels, like on Facebook fanpages, should not be mistaken for social business. Social business is continuous business processes built on social: social marketing, winning new customers through word of mouth; social commerce, customers guiding each other through the sales process by sharing expertise or evaluations; social support, customers helping each other with servicing needs; and of course Crowdsourced Innovation.

Community Platform Architecture

Engagement and enlistment are crucial factors for the success of Crowdsourced Innovation. A vibrant community built on peer-to-peer models sets the foundation for successful implementation. To establish vibrancy, the architecture of the community platform has to be supported by algorithms that are based on gamification and behavioral psychology. Vibrancy is further enhanced by social intelligence, guaranteeing detailed analysis and optimization of the community. For example, for the overall success of the community or the project, key influencers and advocates need to be identified and enabled. To implement social business processes, so-called community apps are required, for example forums, recommendations, competitions or knowledge databases. Through interfaces, these processes can then be integrated into company applications like CRM systems. For the community to become the central point for interactions, user-generated content, and community members, it has to become a social hub by transparently integrating social networks and social channels.

Gabriele Riedmann de Trinidad

Group Director of Business Innovation at METRO

»The times when retailers had the sole function of providing goods are long gone. We now have to understand ourselves as community hubs, bringing together consumers and manufacturers – this is how we identify opportunities for new business models.«

6

THE EMERGENCE OF PLATFORMS FOR OPEN AND CROWDSOURCED INNOVATION

Prof. Kathrin M. Möslein

FAU Erlangen-Nürnberg & HHL Leipzig Graduate School of Management

The previous chapters have already implied the importance of structures to enable Open Innovation and Crowdsourcing processes. Generally, Open and Crowdsourced Innovation build on two basic organizational principles: first, open problem calls that ask for solutions and second, self-selected participation of individuals or teams to solve the challenges posed. Historically, these organizational principles have always existed. However, the emergence of the internet with its interactive possibilities and its detachment from spatiotemporal limitations offers an entirely new dimension. The possibility to form innovation platforms and communities is a central driver for the concept of Crowdsourced Innovation.

Tools as Drivers of Open and Crowdsourced Innovation

Historically, the creation of innovations beyond the boundaries of organizations has always been possible. However, with the growing importance of corporate R&D, the locus of innovative potential was increasingly limited by organizational boundaries. Today, we observe a fundamental change: with the rise of the interactive web, now virtually everyone has the chance to get involved in highly complex innovation activities with large numbers of collaborators on a global scale. These innovation activities are stimulated and supported by a range of specialized tools that form the building blocks for Open Innovation and Crowdsourcing platforms. There are five different classes of tools:

- innovation contests
- innovation markets
- innovation communities
- innovation toolkits
- innovation technologies

The development, diffusion, and implementation of these innovation tools are mainly driven by the attractiveness, usability, and inclusiveness of web 2.0 and social software features. This is evident, when looking at each of the tools, as well as their features and functions in Open Innovation and Crowdsourced Innovation processes.

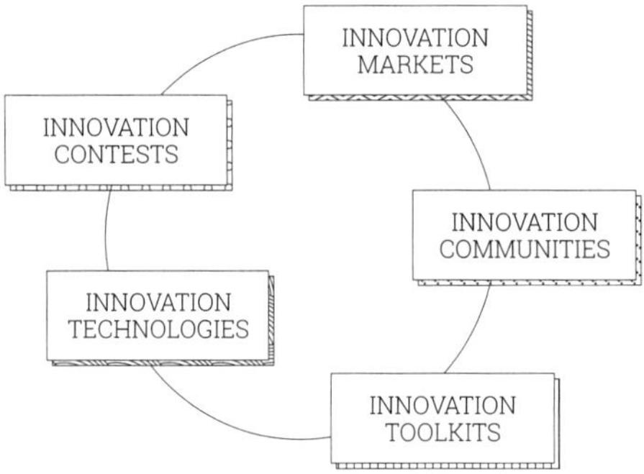

The five different classes of innovation tools that form the building blocks for Open Innovation and Crowdsourcing platforms.

Innovation Contests

Innovation contests in their basic structure have a long-standing tradition and have influenced industries or even societies for a long time. For example, in 1869, Louis Napoleon III of France offered a prize to anyone who could make a "satisfactory substitute for butter, suitable for use by the armed forces and the lower classes"[18] – the birth of margarine. In the 19th century, innovation contests left the realm of political organizers as they were increasingly adopted by industrialists as a powerful means of problem solving. Eventually, during the next century, the realization of innovation contests slowly entered average business.

Compared to these earlier forms, the relevance and the importance of today's innovation contests are enhanced by the internet. Social software features and web 2.0 enable a multitude of actors to announce contests for exciting innovation challenges, with global reach at minimal costs. Considering this aspect, we define an innovation contest as a web-based competition of innovators who use their skills, experiences and creativity to provide a solution for a particular contest challenge defined by an organizer.[19]

Innovation contests are implemented in great variety. The continuum of different contests ranges from simple idea contests to the conception of complex, radical innovations. This includes products, as well as services, solutions or whole business model innovations. The way a challenge is framed and phrased finally decides about the range of innovators attracted, their expertise and motivation. It should be formulated carefully to motivate the right participants without revealing strategic knowledge elements or competence deficits of the organizer.

Innovation Markets

Innovation markets are virtual places, where innovation supply and demand meet. In general, they are realized as web 2.0 supported online platforms, on which innovation seekers (typically organizations) announce innovation challenges and innovation providers (typically individuals or teams of innovators) propose concrete solutions or concepts. Innovation markets act as intermediaries, connecting innovation seekers and innovation providers (often called "solvers").

The example of InnoCentive illustrates the potential of such innovation markets. It was founded in 2001 and declares itself as "the world's first Open Innovation marketplace". Originally focused on innovations in the chemical industry, it now brings together seekers and solvers from all kinds of fields and industries. As of today, InnoCentive reports approximately 300,000 registered "solvers" from nearly 200 countries, a total of more than 1,650 challenges posted with an average success rate of 50% and more than $40 million award money posted.[20]

Innovation Communities

Innovation communities enable innovators to collectively share and develop ideas, discuss concepts, and promote innovations. Web 2.0 and social software based innovation communities normally bundle interested and specialized innovators for particular issues and thus support collective development and enhancement of innovation concepts. The innovation process in such communities is a joint effort, creating a social environment and family-like spirit. Open source software communities are typical examples. The principles of collaborative software development can also be applied to the development of hardware and actual products.

One early example of an innovative, self-organized, and internet-based innovation community can be seen in "the OScar project"[21]: "The idea behind the OScar project is simple: a community of people virtually plans and develops a new car. The idea is about the goal to develop a simple and innovative car, but also about the way how this goal is achieved. We would like to convey the idea of open source to 'hardware' and we want OScar to be the precursor for many different projects in this field." The project was launched in 1999 on the basis of a published manifesto: "To build a car [...] without any factory, any CEO, any funds, any boundaries, [...] but instead with the support of lots of creative people in the web [...] with a global spirit of optimism, [...] representing absolute empowerment. Altogether, this meant to face huge challenges and to use 'the tool' internet in its essential sense." Today, community-based car development is implemented in a highly successful way by Jay Rogers and his team at LocalMotors: the "next-generation, crowd-powered automotive design, manufacturing, and technology to enable the creation of game-changing vehicles"[22].

While in the early days emergent and self-organized communities were the typical pattern for innovation communities, we see today a growing trend in firms utilizing and strategically building such inovation communities for their own specific use.

Innovation Toolkits

Innovation toolkits provide an environment in which users develop solutions step by step. While they can also take on the physical form of an actual innovation package, interactive internet applications now allow an entirely virtual toolkit. Through the application of online configurators for the design of individualized t-shirts or the customization of a new car and its equipment, most consumers are already familiar with the functionalities of this tool. Still, while the application of toolkits is quite widespread for the configuration of predefined products, the application of toolkits for more innovative solutions is still in its infancy.

In order to implement toolkits for Open Innovation on the seeker's as well as on the solver's side efficiently, toolkits have to fulfill five basic requirements[23]:

- Full line of trial and error: Toolkit users tend to be more satisfied with their developed solution, when they can go through the entire cycle of problem solving. This requires that users receive simulated feedback on each step of the development process. Simulations enable users to evaluate the current solution, to improve on it in an iterative process.
- Defined solution space: A toolkit's solution space defines all variations and combinations of feasible solutions. Ideally, the solution space only permits innovation solutions, which take specific technical restrictions into account and are "feasible" from a technical point of view.
- User friendliness: User friendliness describes how users perceive the quality of interaction with the toolkit. The challenge is to find the right degree of complexity (between over-complexity and over-simplicity), openness and

interactivity as to perfectly stimulate the innovators' creativity and motivation.

- Modules and components: Modules and components are the basic building blocks of a toolkit (e.g. visualization, drawing software, text boxes), which make up its operational functionality. Modules and components make up the toolkit's solution space and determine its user friendliness.
- Solution transfer: After its completion, the concept or solution is transferred from the user to a seeker or manufacturer. This toolkit based transfer has to allow for a perfect translation of the solver's or user's solution in the language of the seeker or manufacturer.

Currently utilized toolkits can be broadly classified in three categories, which differ in their strategic goals, design principles, and users to be targeted. Toolkits for User Innovation support the generation of innovation ideas based on a "chemistry kit"-like interface to enable complete trial-and-error cycles, featuring a broad solution space. Toolkits for idea transfer foster application of existing ideas in a new context based on a "black board"-like interface with unlimited solution space. Toolkits for user co-design, by contrast, facilitate product configurations based on a "Lego kit"-like interface, using a restricted solution space and standardized modules. Regardless of specific configurations, toolkit-based innovation requires feedback (either by the system or by users), simulation of possible solutions (regarding design, performance and costs), and encouragement for the quest for solutions.

Innovation Technologies

Innovation technologies enable to progress from concept level of an innovation to prototyping or even production. Innovation technologies comprise all kinds of additive manufacturing technologies (e.g. 3D-printers), but also 3D-scanners or laser cutters. All these technologies are associated with the prospect of an ongoing democratization of innovation activities[24] and with the often proclaimed trend towards personal fabrication. This empowers the users and also changes the traditional, isolated development process within organizations. For example, 3D-printers allow a fast and immediate creation of prototypes during development processes, enabling so-called rapid prototyping. They also allow individuals or organizations to design and produce customized products instantly. Innovators can envision, design, and specify three-dimensional models and print or order them directly from their computers at home.

3D-printers are already available widely, prices are decreasing and usage scenarios are growing. It is obvious that CAD software or 3D-scanners in combination with laser cutters or 3D-printing opens up new possibilities of potential personal production. Similar to our current 2D-printing, we can expect cheap and easy-to-use 3D-printing (and other manufacturing) facilities entering our homes or at least shops around the corner. Such printing labs are already emerging worldwide. Even though they currently target a young generation of hobbyists, they will soon reach a more professional audience of innovators.[25]

Towards Novel Platform Strategies

As a result of internet technologies and web applications, all presented tools for Open and Crowdsourced Innovation include four common and novel effects. They allow

- for large numbers of innovators to contribute,
- empower these innovators to collaborate in widely distributed settings,
- foster high-speed interaction that radically accelerates innovation processes and
- provide a global memory for innovators to build on.

These four effects clearly facilitate collaboration across organizational boundaries and symbolize new opportunities to create innovations. Additionally, the five innovation tools are essentially just building blocks that open up space for novel platform strategies.

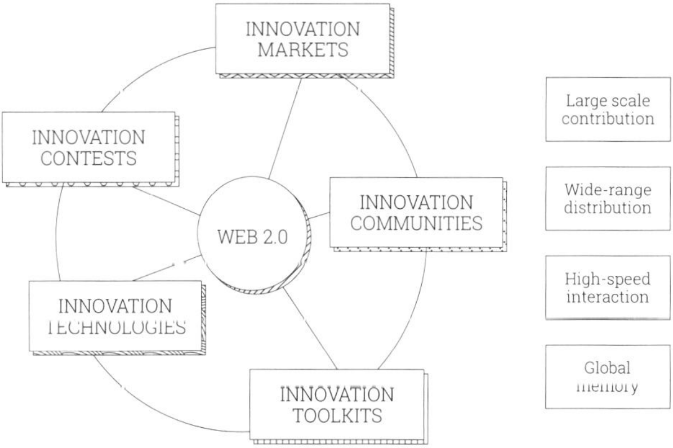

Internet technologies and Web 2.0 applications enable novel forms of platform strategies and collaboration driven by four common effects.

Up to now, these tools have mainly been used separately and often targeted only at a specific audience. For the future, however, we should look at these tools as basic building blocks for Open Innovation and Crowdsourcing platforms. Platforms that fully integrate external individuals into corporate product development and establish a seamless and open process from idea generation to actual production. Combining the building blocks wisely requires a better understanding of their modi operandi, but also of the drivers and barriers of Open Innovation and Crowdsourced Innovation in different kinds of value creation settings. The only way for companies to get this understanding is to collect first-hand experience with the various tools and methods.

Acknowledgement

A very warm thank you to all inside and outside innovators who are part of our ongoing innovation research journey! This chapter bundles knowledge from the research project "Open-I: Open Innovation within Organizations", funded by the federal ministry of research and education (BMBF) and the European social fund (ESF) (support code 01FM07053 and 01FM07054) and builds on earlier work, especially Moeslein & Bansemir (2011)[26]; Moeslein, Huff & Reichwald (2012)[27]; and Moeslein (2013)[28].

Achim Berg

CEO at arvato

»Before the Internet became "social", it was mostly comprised of volatile and anonymous connections. Today, social media platforms establish the necessary structures to make online communication more personal. Platforms for Crowdsourced Innovation should follow this example in order to create lasting relationships and truly collaborative processes.«

7

NEW APPROACHES IN SELECTING THE RIGHT OPEN INNOVATION METHOD

Alexander Lang
CEO at IMAN Solutions

The variety of Open Innovation methods is growing with the ongoing digitalization and the evolving possibilities of the internet. For companies, this means that there is a suitable solution to fit exactly their situation, capabilities, and expectations for innovation projects. But how can one select the right method amongst the different options? In many cases, this is the first obstacle that companies have to face when thinking about implementing Open Innovation strategies. And it is a crucial one. The selection method sets the foundation for the success as well as potential shortcomings and complications of the entire project. This chapter provides a brief outline of factors that should be considered in the selection process and suggests the inclusion of a previously neglected dimension.

The Conventional Selection Process

Typically, when planning the implementation of Crowdsourcing or Open Innovation processes in a company, the factors determining their extent and method are set by the company's specific context, capacities and goals. Among the essential parameters are company size, available monetary budget, time frame, the degree of openness, the scope of application, and the manageable complexity. These factors are mostly quantifiable and objective items, which can be derived from the company's current state. Naturally, matching potential approaches with these factors is an essential step. It is however no guarantee for the success of the project or the quality of the final outcome. Sometimes, Crowdsourcing and Open Innovation do not yield the desired result, even though the method was carefully aligned with the company's parameters. But what is the source of these shortcomings and how can one prevent such flaws?

The Crucial Role of the Project Leader

In most companies Open Innovation projects are performed by an external consultant or an agency and in most cases by one project leader employed by the company carrying out the project. This creates a central bottleneck. The outcome of the project and the implementation of the results will mainly depend on the performance of the project leader. More precisely, it depends on his or her attitude towards the project. Consequently, the method not only has to match the company's parameter, it also has to fit the project leader.

In the newly developed logic (Socially Indicated Match Making Method: SIM3) methods and employees are characterized by sociological criteria following the hypothesis: Methods and people with similar characteristics of criteria are predicted to fit. Not every single participant in an Open Innovation project has to be open, innovative, and curious about new ideas, there are different methods for different kinds of people with different personalities.

Defining and Matching Criteria for Methods and Project Leaders

Matching methods and project leaders requires predefined parameters. They provide the basis on which possible methods are assigned to potential project leaders: a set of the capabilities of the project leaders are compared with the same parameters assigned to the different methods. Those parameters include culture, habits, interaction between participants, or the personality of the employees involved. The following criteria are used to describe methods and the individual project leaders.

OPENNESS

- Individual: receptiveness to new input; communicative ability
- Method: amount of additional input needed; level of communication involved

NATURE OF WORK

- Individual: adaptability to changes; goal-orientation; big-picture perspective
- Method: structure of tasks; level of consistency and stability

RISK

- Individual: risk affinity or risk aversion; dealing with uncertainty and unpredictable outcomes
- Method: level of uncertainty; level of unfamiliarity

ENJOYMENT

- Individual: intrinsic/extrinsic motivation; importance of success and achievement
- Method: perceptibility of success and outcomes; immediacy of interaction and impact

Following the stated hypothesis, potential project leaders and methods can be matched along these criteria. For example, a person characterized as open in terms of receptiveness to new input can be considered more suitable for a method with a high degree of openness than a "closed" person. Following the same argument, a method with high levels of uncertainty might not be the ideal choice, if the project leader is risk averse. The better method and project leaders match along these parameters, the better the matchability and the higher the chances to achieve the desired results. Of course, the fitment rate alone does not guarantee the success of the project. The coupling of method and project leader still has to be suitable for the company's parameters and traditional criteria.

Applying the Matching Process

To put this logic into practice, potential project leaders are interviewed with a standardized questionnaire at the beginning of an Open Innovation project. The questionnaire characterizes the individuals according to the criteria mentioned above. In a second step all methods are characterized by the same set of criteria. In the match making step the methods and the employees are coupled and a prioritized list of matching methods is generated for each decisive project leader. In the last step, using the traditional approach of matching the method to the company's parameters helps to select the best possible couple of method and project leader in order to fulfill the overall project tasks.

As companies very often have only a limited number of project leaders, the qualification of the skills and competencies of each prospective candidate are one way of enlarging the amount of suitable couples. The qualification level of the candidate is constantly increased by training and experience. By doing so the number of possible matches between methods and project leaders will increase. Finally the management picks the coupling, which is most promising to fulfill the company's needs.

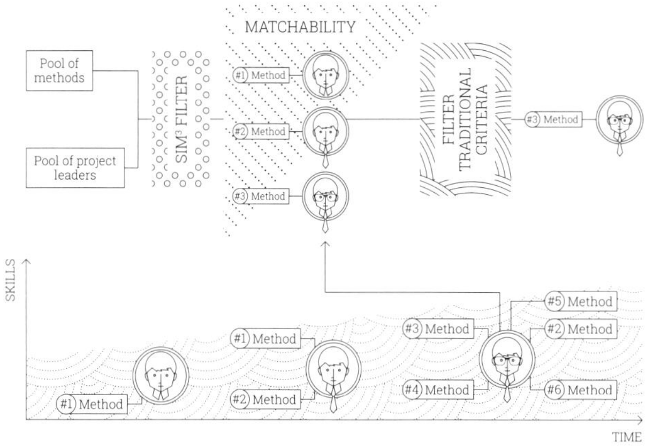

Matching method and project leader is the central part of the new approach. The number of possible methods increases over time with the growing skills of the individual.

Selecting the Right Method: Towards a People Related Approach

Future research will concentrate on a more organizational aspect. Looking at the problem from a different angle, not only methods can be selected but also employees, who then perform the projects and implement the results. Following this logic, the problem dictates the Open Innovation method used, but the method dictates the person who should be involved. Instead of qualifying existing employees, using internal resources only, opening the organizations, using external resources, e.g. retired ex-employees, students, start-ups, external companies, or engineering services might also be a suitable approach. In the near future, the development of an open employment market with the right person for a particular project from external sources could be a solution.

The newly developed logic (SIM3) reduces the risk in Open Innovation projects by matching the right method to the employees involved. Companies will be able to absorb the acquired knowledge better and the projects will have a higher probability of success. The new logic changes the selection process for the Open Innovation method from a problem-related to a people-related approach.

Dr. Armin Pfoh

Vice President Corporate Innovation Management at TÜV Süd

»The great thing about Crowdsourced Innovation is its potential to find the unknown. Ideas, needs, or solutions you were not looking for in the first place. We have worked on a new business model in the area of smart factories and were able to get in touch with many factory workers who brainstormed new ideas with us.«

8

ADDING VALUE TO SOCIAL MEDIA WITH CROWDSOURCING

Matias Roskos

Community Manager at ProSiebenSat.1 Digital

The rise of social media irrevocably changed the landscape of the internet. Users adapted their usage patterns accordingly and created a truly social web. And while many social media platforms and other communication channels have grown to facilitate communication and interaction, the basis of the social web remains the daily practiced communication of the users connecting with each other. In order to successfully harness the social web to align with and drive business objectives, companies must understand that users drive social media by communicating, interacting, and connecting with each other, exchanging ideas, opinions, and emotions. Many companies view the social web as nothing more than a platform for advertisements, ultimately adding little or no value. Instead, a successful social media strategy positions the social web for what it really is: a two-way street of communication and interaction between a company and the users.

A new Culture of Interaction in the Social Web

Crowdsourcing takes advantage of this new communicative and interactive culture. Strategically planned and coordinated Crowdsourcing can help a company turn social media activities into strategic competitive advantages. Gone are the days when companies could only speak to consumers through advertisements and dedicated market research activities. The biggest appeal of Crowdsourcing is its ability to involve existing or future customers, turning passive advocates and fans into (inter-)active communities.

Stronger relationships with consumers is the first strategic advantage of Crowdsourced Innovation. Meaningful campaigns strengthen – and in some cases create for the first time – reciprocal communication between companies and their current and future customers. Crowdsourced Innovation enables companies to ask consumers specific questions about existing products and services, but it also serves as a forum for consumers to tell companies their currently unmet needs and desires. When a company uses Crowdsourcing to elicit these ideas from customers and then acts on this data, customers feel heard, included, and valued as a trusted advisor. Individual consumers not only enjoy the new product or find it useful, they also identify with it. The black box environment surrounding the development process is demystified and the effect of their input is visible in new products or services. As a consequence, consumers and especially customers feel closer to the product or service and thus are more loyal to the company that developed the product or service with their support.

Enriching Social Media

Crowdsourcing also positively affects the online presence of a company. Successful projects draw all types of media attention. When Crowdsourcing campaigns take place on social media platforms, participants can easily share the project and their activity with friends by posting or tweeting about it. When participants feel engaged in the project and excited about the product or service, they are likely to recruit friends and followers to participate online and rave about the project offline, too. Crowdsourcing projects should also be closely aligned with the overall media strategy of the company: some projects are an excellent vehicle to recruit relevant and popular bloggers to participate and create a buzz among their readers. More traditional avenues such as relevant newspapers, magazines, and TV channels can also spread the news of the project. Data gathered from such a comprehensive media strategy is also useful for search engine optimization.

Companies that successfully implement a Crowdsourcing campaign often enhance their image and strengthen their brand identity. Through a robust social web presence a company demonstrates strong ties with its customers and the willingness to serve their needs. By using new and popular channels like Facebook, Twitter, and Instagram a company proves its relevancy to the market while at the same time including these vehicles in its overall marketing and communication strategy. Opening up their development processes paves the way to innovation, strengthening a brand image linked to innovative products and services. Furthermore, customers are included directly into the marketing activities at a very early stage; they feel like they are spreading insider information as soon as the product, its name, its packaging, or its image campaign begins to take form.

A Crowdsourcing project increases customer loyalty, expands the existing online presence, and strengthens the image of the company. More importantly, it is a great learning experience and an opportunity to get unexpected user insights. Crowdsourcing campaigns allow a business to become an active component in an ever-developing and fast-changing communication landscape. Crowdsourcing helps a company to keep its finger on the pulse of its customers and the wider audience of the social web: it may even influence the direction of both. Crowdsourcing also uncovers hidden desires, needs, and opinions of customers that traditional market research cannot tap or reveal. As a direct result, companies have created a much faster feedback loop regarding changing market environments and are able to develop products and services that fulfill customer needs better and faster.

Through strategic social media campaigns Crowdsourced Innovation adds value for a company as part of a coordinated communication strategy. Crowdsourcing utilizes the social web much more effectively and comprehensively than conventional social media marketing. The success of crowdsourced products can be proven via a measurable increase in revenue and/or margin or customer satisfaction. Further quantifiable success factors like the number of users involved or newly generated ideas can be tracked easily and are a major strength of Crowdsourcing campaigns. Companies can define more precise objectives and key performance indicators to improve their social media marketing and product development strategies. With clearer goals and better metrics, companies can get ahead or even leapfrog competition while at the same time moving closer to their existing and new customers.

Christoph Bornschein
CEO at TLGG

»As customers are losing trust in institutions and corporations they increasingly rely on the opinions of their friends. Companies have to get actively involved in this communication – instead of using social media as yet another channel to push their messages.«

9

PLEASE ELABORATE

MODERATING CROWDSOURCING COMMUNITIES

The most fertile ground for innovative ideas and promising product and services is wherever diverse people communicate with each other. Based on our experience, implementing successful Crowdsourcing projects depends on effective management of the people involved and not just technologies or platforms. Rarely do new product or service concepts simply emerge from connecting users to each other; online Crowdsourcing communities need to be managed and guided towards a common goal in order to deliver tangible results.

Online communities however face many inherent challenges. Most groups are composed of many heterogeneous individuals, who have no personal connection amongst each other. They have come together in a virtual space where their interactions are limited almost exclusively to text and media attachments. They are often biased towards their own ideas, which they initially perceive as superior to all others. In addition they tend to articulate themselves with unclear or ambiguous comments, off-topic remarks, and sometimes non-productive criticism. The key question in such a complex environment is to ensure a successful final outcome of Crowdsourced Innovation. The answer lies in effective community management.

Successful community management harnesses the creative power of a diverse group of participants and directs the interaction towards the final goal of the project. In the end, the only common element that a Crowdsourcing community has is its final purpose. Considering the lack of personal relationships and face-to-face communication, the common goal is the essential glue that holds the community together.

At the same time, successful community managers also cultivate creative freedom to ensure an innovative and unique outcome.

Actively Driving the Agenda

Due to the goal-oriented nature, Crowdsourcing communities must be managed differently from other online forums and platforms. Typically, community management is focused on keeping a calm and politically correct environment. It is reactive, only intervening to stop arguments or violations. Moderators act as an authority, managing top-down when required. Community management in Crowdsourcing, however, demands a more collaborative approach and higher levels of anticipation and guidance. The moderator needs to interact and be perceived on eye level with the participants to facilitate communication and to drive the community successfully to its goal.

The first step in successful community management is to set and communicate simple and straightforward guidelines, which all members of the community should adhere to. We recommend to clearly communicate the six principles shown in the following illustration upfront and in a transparent manner:

Once all users are aware of and adhere to these guidelines, the real community management starts. In order to drive a Crowdsourcing community towards its final objective and nurture the creative freedom required for an innovative outcome, the community manager needs to focus on the details, support by visualizing submitted ideas, cultivate constructive criticism, consolidate similar ideas and allow participants to share their knowledge and skills.

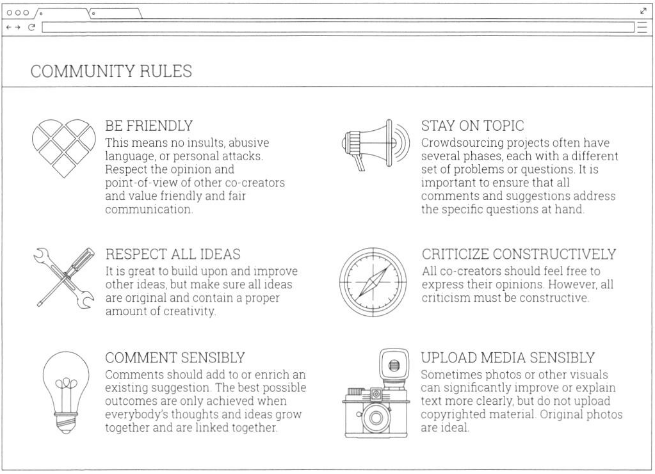

The six important principles and guidelines for the interaction within the community are the foundation for goal-oriented and innovative collaboration.

The role of moderating Crowdsourcing communities is divided into two general types: general moderation and expert moderation. Individuals with different qualifications can manage these two types of moderation separately. We have also seen situations where the general moderator can handle the entire project by discussing the relevant subject-specific questions with an expert about once a week.

THE GENERAL MODERATOR

- Monitors the community to limit and resolve disagreements or incongruities
- Answers questions about the nuts and bolts of the project
- Asks probing and clarifying questions about submissions
- Combines duplicate submissions

THE EXPERT MODERATOR

- Adds technical context to the submissions
- Asks specific and precise technical questions
- Answers the community's subject-specific questions

Our recipe for unleashing the creative potential of a community by stimulating imagination, supporting ideas, and challenging common opinions are the following five moderation principles.

- Probe for details
- Bring submitted ideas to life
- Cultivate constructive criticism
- Consolidate similar ideas
- Enable participants to share their skills

Probe for Details

One of the most important practices a community manager can do is ask for more details. Often a co-creator will describe an idea in a short and hasty comment. The community manager should follow up with targeted questions that will lead to better insights and more useful information. More importantly this practice opens the door for other participants to get involved. This is key, because Crowdsourcing is mostly successful when ideas are developed from many diverse people utilizing their unique background, knowledge, and experience. Sometimes participants consider it disrespectful to rework ideas of others. In this situation, the moderator needs to signal through encouraging comments that collaboration is not only desired, but that it is in the best interest of the community. The moderator should thus not pose questions to a single participant; he/she should open it up to the entire community, even when the responses are only relevant for a specific idea of an individual person.

Furthermore, detailed and thoughtful follow-up questions show honest interest in an idea of a participant. Skillful moderation and specific follow-up questions establish a culture of respect and relevance within the community for the task at hand. However, we have seen many moderators falling into the trap of thanking participants for every single submission with standard verbiage like "Thank you for your idea". This practice should not be overused, because such cut-and-paste, automated compliments devalue the time and effort participants put into their contributions.

The conversation below is a positive example how a moderator successfully probes for details while opening up the conversation to a larger group. This interaction occurred during one of our projects with Yello Strom, a German energy provider. A participant stated: "In an ideal situation, I envision something like a question-and-answer forum or chat room where you can ask urgent questions and receive an answer within a few days." The moderator reacted instantly: "I have a question for all participants: Would you envision such a customer forum to be more of a community for the general exchange of information or a 'customer-helps-customer' forum where specific problems are stated and answered? In both scenarios the key question is: What is the benefit for me as a customer from such a forum? Either being the person asking a question or the person answering? We are eager to hear your opinion – thanks for the great suggestion!"

Bring Submitted Ideas to Life

Crowdsourced Innovation aims to reach participants who have specific knowledge or experience with methods and solutions that are currently not present within the company. This does not mean, however, that these participants have the ability to convey their ideas and suggestions through visual concepts. Our experience shows that the majority of suggestions is usually submitted as text, but a moderator can support participants by getting a graphic designer to draw a mock-up of the idea and by asking "Is this what you had in mind?". Such visualizations trigger very productive and fruitful discussions focusing on details and design. The moderator simply needs to have someone at hand who can quickly and effectively sketch a picture with all the relevant elements. The example to the right demonstrates a situation where two iterations of a visual were required until the relevant company stakeholders understood what the participant had in mind.

This approach uncovers and transfers knowledge into the organization and, above all, makes the information accessible to internal stakeholders. This way the "not-invented-here" resistance can be avoided; crowdsourced material becomes more useful and insightful to internal stakeholders when the submitted ideas and suggestions are depicted in a format the internal team is familiar with. Integrating tools like configurators into the Crowdsourcing project is another possibility to help participants visualize and demonstrate their ideas. Specifically assembled kits that enable users to create prototypes are a great example of this method.

♡ I would like to have an improved cup holder for the back seat. With the
2 current system, even small water bottles don't fit. Maybe it is possible to integrate such a system for holding bottles into the backrest of the front seats.

6 Comments Share Report

COMMUNITY MODERATOR, 1 day ago

Dear Daniela, we tried to visualize your suggestion. Does this picture match your idea and the concept you have imagined? This system can easily hold larger bottles at the back of the front seats.

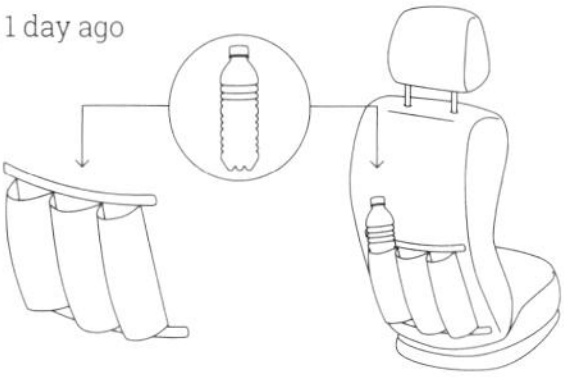

DANIELA, 1 day ago

Actually, I was thinking more of a foldable tray, like in planes. It should have adjustable rings to hold all sorts of drinks safely in place, e.g. coffee.

COMMUNITY MODERATOR, 2 hours ago

Thanks for clarifying! Here is a new picture. Does it show your idea better than the last one? The tray can be folded and the holders are adjustable to tightly fit around any cups or bottles.

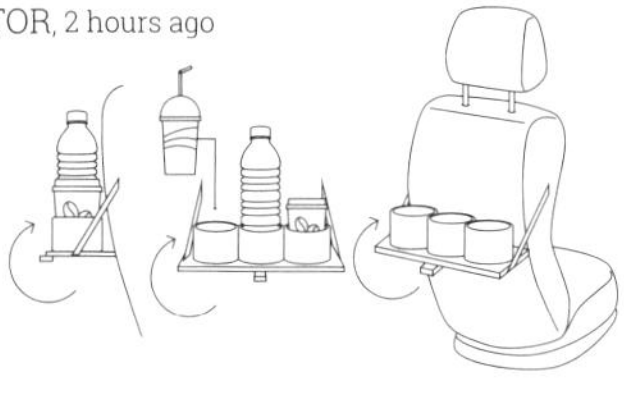

DANIELA, 1 hour ago

Yes! This looks great. I think it is really important that these rings really grab the cups, so they don't fall over when the car turns sharply.

Visualizing ideas that are too complex to descibe in a few words can facilitate the transfer of knowledge, as we did in this example in a project with Ford Germany.

Cultivate Constructive Criticism

Keeping a positive tone is key for a Crowdsourcing forum. However, some participants tend to comment on every suggestion with negative phrases like "I don't really like this" or "This isn't that good". Often their objective is simply to join the conversation, make complaints, attract attention, or – when applicable – earn rewards. Such an approach however violates the community rules, explicitly asking for constructive criticism. Thoughtful criticism always offers a suggestion for improvement or an alternative approach to the problem. This method is based on established brainstorming guidelines, where a simple "That won't work," can limit the group's creativity and make other participants think twice about posting very creative and sometimes unusual or exceptional suggestions. Therefore, it is important to mitigate such comments by subtly referring to the community rules even when nothing overtly insulting or offensive has been said. The goal is to establish the community forum as a nurturing environment for the incubation of all ideas. When a moderator makes sure that all community members follow this rule, a positive and creative community climate is in place. It is very important that the participants feel immersed in a positive environment, where they can offer up crazy thoughts or nascent ideas to the community for improvement and further development.

Consolidate Similar Ideas

Even in well-planned and structured Crowdsourcing projects, participants often submit duplicate suggestions. This can irritate participants who are deeply engaged and very familiar with the project, but even worse, the best ideas are sometimes cluttered and do not rise to the top. When duplicate ideas are posted in two different streams, participants will split their votes, comments, and suggestions between the two. This may lead to a misrepresentation of the best ideas with the strongest support. Therefore, we highly recommend to quickly consolidate similar or almost equal suggestions. For example, a similar but slightly differing suggestion can be added to an earlier suggestion as an improvement, point of development, or even a more precise element.

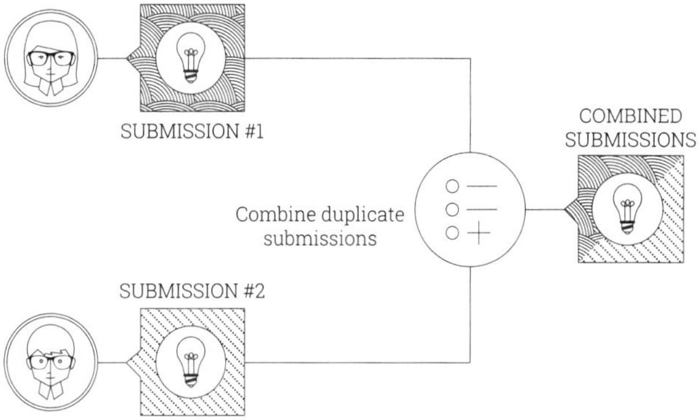

Similar suggestions should be identified and combined to one single idea in order to foster discussion and a collaborative, creative process within the community.

As a basic rule, moderators should consolidate and combine similar suggestions as soon as possible. Otherwise many votes and comments will accumulate around two separate submissions moving the same basic idea into two different directions. Consolidating ideas later in the process will only cause confusion and frustration among participants. When merging duplicate suggestions a key focus should be to ensure that the project software combines the accumulated votes of both suggestions. Furthermore, sophisticated project software can assist the moderator and augment the content with automated semantic algorithms, merging duplicate suggestions.

Enable Participants to Share Their Skills

The feeling you get when you create something new or ingenious is special; you want to run and tell all your friends. Crowdsourcing participants feel the same way. Thus a Crowdsourcing project platform needs to be open to all interested parties, allow participants to share their creations, and encourage external curiosity. Furthermore, it is important to incorporate functions into the Crowdsourcing platform that enable idea sharing. The exact functions depend on the specific platform type: Facebook share pop-ups work well after the submission of an idea in a consumer goods project; however, when primarily targeting professionals it is better to integrate sharing functions from LinkedIn and XING. Alternatively, Pinterest is better suited for a project requiring a lot of visual content.

Some projects with very specific and tight timeframes can use existing social media platforms without any add-ons for the submission of ideas, for example, with a specific hashtag on Twitter. The downside to this approach, however, is that participants do not have to register for a project-specific platform and do not have to agree to project-specific terms and conditions. Thus the question regarding the legal right of use of the submitted ideas remains unclear. Therefore, we recommend a mandatory registration process for anyone intending to contribute.

Enhancing the Toolkit

In Crowdsourced Innovation projects the response time for questions and comments is not expected to be as short as in other areas of social media. This results from the fact that participants do not view the platform as a venue for assistance or complaints. We recommend checking submissions twice a day (late in the morning and early in the evening), in order to address potential areas of concern early and divert negative discussions to a specific one on one side conversation. If criticisms of the company, complaints about a particular incident, or similar comments find their way into the Crowdsourcing platform, the user in question should be referred to the appropriate team or contact person to address, own, and solve the complaint. Shortly thereafter those comments should be deleted stating something like the following: "Please direct your comment to Mr. Snyder in our customer call center and he will be happy to assist you further. Since this forum is meant for a discussion about a new type of nail polish, I will remove your comment."

Automated emails alerting users regarding new comments or ideas on their original suggestions or highlighting the consolidation of their idea with another concept are another way to advance and support the moderation process.

The centerpiece of any Crowdsourced Innovation approach is the organically growing community of diverse and creative individuals, held together by a common objective. Without guidelines and careful management, however, Crowdsourcing communities cannot reach their full potential. Managing a community well is a delicate, but absolutely critical task. The best and most successful community managers work in close alignment with platform technologies while at the same time emphasizing and managing the human element of the project. Having this in mind, the results will be feasible and a success.

Xiaoqun Clever

Chief Technology Officer at ProSiebenSat.1 Media

»Our viewers are constantly commenting, recommending, and talking about TV shows; this hasn't changed during the past 30 years. Nowadays technologies enable us to be more engaged with our target audiences, to listen to them, to capture the conversations, to actively participate, and even to utilize this user generated content to reshape our programmings.«

10

THE CROWDSOURCED INNOVATION CANVAS

When planning a Crowdsourced Innovation approach, it is of utmost importance to start with a holistic approach that includes different aspects and discovers potential trade-offs. We have designed and built the "Crowdsourced Innovation Canvas" based on the Business Model Canvas supporting your strategic decision-making. The Business Model Canvas is a management template for documenting existing and creating new business models, which was initially proposed by Alexander Osterwalder[29].

The Crowdsourced Innovation Canvas is a visualization of a framework that allows you to plan, conceptualize, question, and adjust your collaborative innovation strategy. An interactive workshop is the ideal set up for working with the canvas. From our experience, working in small teams of up to seven people drives the most creative results. We typically use a poster-sized (A0) layout to collaboratively add content using sticky notes to capture different ideas. When planning platforms with our clients, we address the following parameters:

CROWD: WHO ARE THE RELEVANT PARTICIPANTS?

- Describe the different types of expected participants.
- What is the motivation of the various groups?
- How can individual groups of participants be reached best and what are appropriate channels?

GOALS: WHAT DO YOU WANT TO ACHIEVE AND HOW DO YOU MEASURE IT?

- Which specific goals define success in your business already and how can they be applied to your Crowdsourced Innovation strategy?

- In what timeframe do you want to achieve these goals?
- How can you measure your goals? Which key performance indicators are relevant?

RESULTS: WHAT KIND OF SUBMISSIONS DO YOU EXPECT FROM YOUR PARTICIPANTS?

- What is the format for the input? How shall the co-creators contribute? Do you want to use a configurator, free text submissions or other means?
- Which insights do you want to gain from the results?
- How do you want to link submissions to your brand?

PROBLEM: WHAT IS THE KEY ISSUE THAT SHOULD BE SOLVED BY THE COMMUNITY?

- Describe current questions, problems and needs that should be addressed and solved.
- Who is affected by this problem and who benefits from a potential solution?
- How is the problem addressed currently? Are there workarounds in place?

CHALLENGES: WHAT OBSTACLES DO YOU HAVE TO OVERCOME?

- Which questions have to be answered before starting?
- Are there any challenges or risks and how can they be evaluated or mitigated?

TEAM: WHO NEEDS TO BE INVOLVED AND INFORMED?

- Which internal stakeholders need to be involved? Who will be part of the project team and who needs to be regularly informed about the progress?

- Which external partners and stakeholders are required for the operational implementation?
- Which partners can accelerate the project? Who can serve as a multiplier?

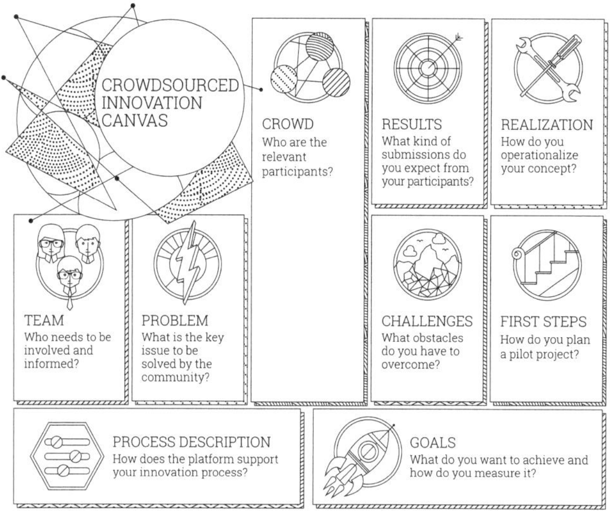

The innosabi Crowdsourced Innovation Canvas allows you to plan, conceptualize, and adjust your collaborative innovation strategy. (based on: Osterwalder, 2014[vi])

REALIZATION: HOW DO YOU OPERATIONALIZE YOUR CONCEPT?

- Are there important organizational interfaces to be considered?
- What kind of technology will you use for the implementation?
- How do you implement the project into existing systems?

FIRST STEPS: HOW DO YOU PLAN A PILOT PROJECT?

- How can you apply learnings from your existing projects to your Crowdsourced Innovation approach?

- Where and when can you discuss your approach with the target audience?
- What could be first steps towards the realization?

PROCESS DESCRIPTION: HOW DOES THE PLATFORM SUPPORT YOUR INNOVATION PROCESS?

- How do you address an innovation question?
- Is it possible to break down a core-question into several sub-questions?
- Which steps define the project? Are there sub-steps?

Dr. Michael Gebert

Partner at Crowd Mentor Network

»Without a doubt, constant reflection and innovation is crucial for the success of every business. With the power of heterogenous knowledge pools and crowds of talented individuals, Crowdsourcing sets future standards for interactive value creation and successful Open Innovation.«

11 IMPLEMENTING CROWDSOURCED INNOVATION A GUIDE

For many of our clients, the initial intention is to generate as many ideas as possible via a Crowdsourced Innovation strategy. However, we have found it to be of utmost importance to focus on finding the RIGHT ideas. Companies have to understand and define the potential benefits of working together with customers and users. Together with our clients we first determine the objectives of this strategy: they have to be in line with the image of the company, the degree of innovation (incremental or disruptive) and within the parameters of the project (feasibility, time, and budget). The following key questions are examples for starting a discussion:

- Are the participants involved in developing a completely new product or service, which has never been seen before, or should they help create a product or service that extends an existing line and can be completed easily within strict parameters?
- Do we want to generate new ideas based on customer experiences with existing products, or do we want to identify user needs that are currently not satisfied by existing products?
- How do you implement and operationalize the result; e.g. how much influence does the winning idea have in the development process of the new product or service?

Once the objectives of the project have been defined, it will become clear which internal departments need to be involved. Just as Crowdsourced Innovation crosses the boundaries between companies and external parties, it also crosses the internal boundaries drawn by departments and their various responsibilities. It unfolds its full potential, when all internal parties are given the chance to contribute their specific expertise to the project. Working with a community to generate ideas and to solve problems often requires support from the research and development division. On the other hand the task of the marketing and communications department is to recruit participants and to communicate the platform to relevant media and partners as well as in social media. Product managers are very important for defining the technical and branding framework as well as planning the product launch. A quick check with the legal department and employees responsible for corporate identity is also highly recommended. Additionally, a Crowdsourced Innovation project requires a team responsible for moderating the community and for monitoring the progress of the project. The project manager of this team should be from the marketing, product management or innovation department, depending on the scope of the project and the organizational structure of the company.

Once this interdisciplinary team has been assembled, the next step is to define parameters for the future product or service. If the goal of the project is to achieve a high degree of innovation, then the parameters should be oriented around broad, company-wide objectives or overarching questions (e.g. "How will changing consumer demographics affect our products?"). If the degree of the desired innovation is rather low, then the feasibility of production processes and the respective implementation are often the limiting factors. If, for example, the goal is to create a crowdsourced shower gel and to get it to market within six months, then easily modifiable characteristics like fragrance, color, or label design can be determined by the participants. In such a situation, however, the project and the following new product are most likely not going to try to alter the showering habits of the participants.

A goal-oriented project with a relatively high probability of success requires a detailed and specific list of questions for the participants that drive creative yet implementable answers. These questions need to state clearly to everyone involved the expectations of the company for the project. They should also be detailed enough to encourage relevant input as well as exciting enough to drive creative, unconventional, and unexpected submissions.

Understanding Platform Requirements

Every company interested in Crowdsourced Innovation should utilize a technical platform, which serves as the foundation for collaborative and innovative input from their customers. This platform acts as the intermediary between the company and customers creating a space where suggestions are voiced, ideas are discussed, and innovative concepts are developed further. Ideally Crowdsourced Innovation platforms ensure two complimentary aspects:

First, the platform creates a welcoming and motivating environment that invites users to share their ideas in a creative and playful manner. The design of the platform is vital in creating a relaxed atmosphere that does not look and feel like a bureaucratic suggestion template. The platform should also be intuitive, so that participants can submit their ideas to the community without having to first jump through complex technical hoops and user manuals.

The second essential aspect is the platform's ability to transparently display all necessary information and parameters that drive idea generation. For example, the innovation topic and the task of the co-creators must be stated in an easily understandable way. Furthermore, the platform must be able to display the entire process from the generation of ideas to the selection of the best ideas and finally towards the specific implementation of the most promising concepts. The course of the project should therefore follow a so-called Stage Gate innovation process whereby ideas only proceed to the next step if they have successfully passed the criteria of the previous gate. A review process anchored between any two steps makes sure that an idea meets all the specific requirements to proceed from one step to the next. During the first step participants can discuss and exchange ideas freely. Before they can vote for the most promising and popular ideas, the project manager needs to coordinate internal approval of the highest rated ideas regarding plausibility, feasibility, and desirability.

Use Configurators Wisely

Many companies who want to implement Crowdsourced Innovation for the first time opt for a configurator – a tool that allows users to customize products by mixing and matching interchangeable elements from a predefined set. This mechanism has been predominantly used in projects resulting in custom-built, built-to-order products like chocolate, computers, automobiles, and furniture. This mass customization stands in contrast to the use of a

IMPLEMENTING
CROWDSOURCED INNOVATION

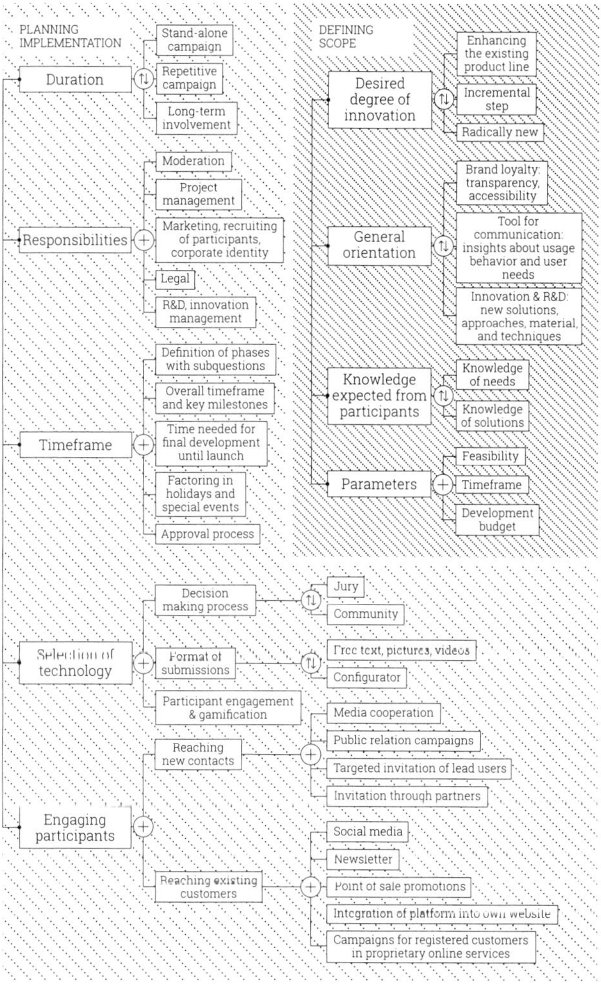

Many different aspects need to be considered when planning and implementing Crowdsourced Innovation platforms as part of a holistic strategy.

configurator in a Crowdsourced Innovation approach, where the main goal is to develop a single, mass marketable product. The key difference is, that the final product development is based on the preferences voiced by the community rather than customizing an individual product for the user.

Crowdsourcing campaigns that use configurators are often supported by an extensive marketing effort and thereby achieve a high level of publicity. While a configurator is great at delivering feasible products and marketplace buzz, it is only one of many different ways to implement Crowdsourced Innovation effectively. A configurator that limits the options to predetermined combinations provides companies with a relatively high level of control over the potential results and their feasibility. For companies who want to enhance the communication with their customers by quickly producing and selling a collaboratively created product, the configurator method provides the required predictability for planning purposes. Only readily available elements or ingredients are listed as possible choices, so that solely feasible combinations make their way into the configurator – thus the risk that the crowd selects or develops a non-feasible product is almost completely eliminated.

Because of the high level of standardization inherent in a configurator, a large number of entries can be processed with limited extra cost or effort. Campaigns can get millions of entries: the British potato chip brand "Walkers" initiated its "Do us a flavour" Crowdsourcing campaign and received 1,213,853 suggestions for a new potato chip flavor within six weeks[30]. Moderating this amount of entries manually is not feasible, but a configurator gives a useful overview of the results from such large pools of data. There is a great wealth of specific information in this data that can be collected and used: reviewing the combinations chosen by customers allows to identify the clear preferences of specific target groups for different variations and combinations.

If the goal of the Crowdsourcing project is to generate novel insights and to ignite or kick-start an innovative product development cycle, a configurator can considerably limit the creativity and novelty of submissions. In order to achieve a meaningful innovation approach and to receive truly unique ideas – Crowdsourced Innovation's greatest raison d'etre – the unforeseeable must be allowed to happen. A configurator, however, limits the amount of the unexpected or unknown significantly.

Motivating and Incentivizing

After the goals have been defined and a platform has been chosen, a company needs to define the target group of participants and how to engage them. Potential co-creators cannot only be found amongst existing customers and great ideas originate in many different places. This is why the recruitment of participants should focus on a diverse mix of sources, reaching existing customers as well as previously unidentified and uninvolved individuals.

- REACHING EXISTING CUSTOMERS: Use of social media, newsletters, point of sale promotions, integration of platform into own website, campaigns for registered customers in proprietary online services.

- REACHING NEW CONTACTS: Use of media cooperations, public relation campaigns, targeted invitations of lead users, invitations through partners.

Defining a strategy for building a relevant community is essential. Merging viewpoints and ideas of multiple co-creators with different experiences sets the stage for the most innovative ideas. A single person rarely comes up with a truly revolutionary idea; instead great ideas are shaped in dialogues and emerge from swarm intelligence.

Understanding the motivation of participants to join a Crowdsourced Innovation community is of central importance to the project and one of the essential factors for success. Their key motives are often idealistic and non-monetary: co-creators decide to participate because they want to express their specific product wishes, suggestions for improvement, or a desire to have fun while innovating with others. Crowdsourced Innovation projects are often very successful because the participants feel intrinsically motivated by a yearning to use their innovative capacity for the common cause. Often participants do not expect any kind of compensation for their work as co-creators. They feel highly valued when a company gives them the opportunity to collaborate creating a new product they value and use. Not just designing a product to suit one's own needs, but instead creating a product that can help many users is one of the greatest motivation factors a Crowdsourcing participant can experience. Co-creators primarily want to be heard and to be taken seriously by a company. Thus we recommend to always put this principle at the center when planning incentives.

Intrinsic motivation can be undermined by monetary compensation; nevertheless co-developers should be rewarded as a means of appreciation in order to maintain a fair environment in Crowdsourced Innovation approaches. Compensation and rewards should always be based on the quality (evaluated by a jury and/or peer-to-peer rating mechanisms) as well as the quantity of the contribution from the participants. It is appropriate to offer the newly developed product as a non-monetary reward, which will also drive excitement for the new product. Other ideas for incentivizing co-developers include special roles in the community (e.g. the opportunity to influence the final decision on a particular product feature), a coupon or voucher for other products or services of the company, or an offer for an internship or assignment in the department of the company that hosted the Crowdsourcing project.

Phases of a Crowdsourced Innovation Project

We have seen that the most successful projects are the ones that follow the Stage Gate innovation process. This means that the overarching innovation question should be divided into individual consecutive sub-questions. This way the answer to one sub-question provides the starting point for the discussion of the next question enabling a continuous development process driving tangible results. Asking multiple sub-questions ensures that the final outcome contains the ideas of many participants with different competences and backgrounds. Only such a set up implements a collaborative, community-driven approach instead of a competitive one, where one single person submits a winning proposition and everybody else feels like losing.

Projects are particularly successful when the questions during the different phases progress from general to specific content. We suggest starting with questions addressing needs or user problems to be solved. Examples are: "What problem or problems need to be solved?" or "What are the needs of consumers that are currently not addressed by existing products on the market?". After receiving useful replies, more specific topics such as technology, form, or design of a solution can be addressed. Finally, questions regarding the packaging and marketing of the product should be asked. This process can also be implemented in an iterative way. The concept of a Stage Gate process not only allows for a clearly defined and logical process, it also enables the company to exercise an approval process: for example, a company will only release the winning suggestions to the next round if all the relevant parameters such as technical feasibility and/or brand coherence are satisfied.

However, such a decision making process must be communicated upfront to all participants very openly and clearly – false expectations can quickly lead to frustration and disappointment within the community. Key questions are: "When does the jury or the community decide?" or "When does a voting take place and which results are shared?". It is very important that specific eligibility requirements are stated and provide the framework for a detailed description of the decision making process. The method also needs to be communicated clearly to the key stakeholders in the company so no one feels excluded or disrespected.

A precise project plan should adhere to the following principles:

- Defining the scope and timeline for the project
- Clearly stating the different phases during the project
- Defining the relevant decision makers and the timing of the approval process
- Setting key milestones

After the overall structure of the project, the exact project trajectory, and the respective phases have been defined, the specific method and format of the submission of the ideas must be envisioned and tested, subject to the parameters and objectives of the project:

- If the goal of the project is very specific and pre-defined, then a configurator is a good choice. A configurator displays a range of options that participants can pick and choose from to design a final product. The different suggestions are automatically visualized combining predefined elements into a final picture.
- If the project parameters are very open and the goal of the Crowdsourcing project requires a large degree of innovation, it is best to avoid a predefined context. Instead we recommend free format suggestions such as free text, pictures, or videos. Indexing options can be linked to these suggestions so overarching themes and common features can be easily recognized and related content can be automatically connected. For example, if an idea is submitted as a solution to a particular medical problem on a platform focused on healthcare innovation, it can be tagged with the name of

body part that is affected, the situation in which the problem arises, or the related disease. This way connected ideas can be recognized and organized across a platform – a cure for back pain, for example, detected in a discussion regarding sport injuries might also be applicable to a different discussion on problems whilst working in an office environment.

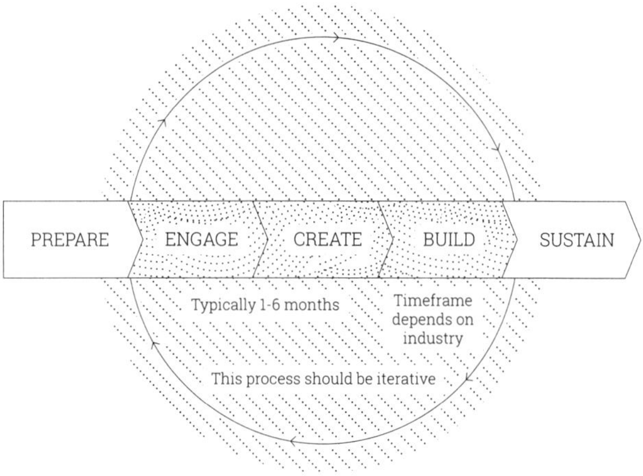

The process of Crowdsourced Innovation projects should be iterative. Participants should be involved repeatedly to ensure sustainable results and success.

Active Participation

The simpler it is to participate, the more likely users will be to actively engage. We suggest to design areas for input of the community similar to respective fields used on social media platforms: a single box with room for a few lines of text instead of a detailed questionnaire with multiple fields is preferred. Furthermore, the display of the suggestions should reflect a level of imperfection, so the community perceives the importance of continuing to gather and develop ideas. The more complete, specific, or polished an idea the less likely other participants are willing to add to or enhance the idea. Crowdsourced Innovation delivers the best results when people with different ideas and varied backgrounds come together, connect, and discuss ideas capitalizing on the sum of their work rather than driving individual efforts.

Finally it needs to be decided, at what point in time and whether it is appropriate at all for participants to comment on submitted suggestions. Discussions surrounding suggestions and comments often spark new insights. In particular, customer comments often encourage the further development of suggestions. In spite of all these advantages, it can make sense to eliminate a comment function for efficiency purposes since managing comments requires thoughtful and often time intensive moderation. In specific situations – where confidentiality is extremely important – we advise to limit the visibility of submissions to the origniator of the content and to the moderator who has full transparency in the background.

Long-term Orientation

When a Crowdsourcing project achieves its objective successfully, the relationship between the company and its customers should not end. An important premise of Crowdsourcing in product development is to encourage and maintain a long-term, cooperative, and constructive relationship. The collaborative development of a new product is ideally only a highlight and potentially a starting point of a much longer, sustainable customer-manufacturer relationship.

When designing new products, companies can easily and quickly revert to an established and proven community of co-developers. Even if there is no urgent need for a new product, the knowledge and ideas of co-creators can be used to stay close to new market trends and untapped customer needs. Such a proactive dialogue signals to existing and also to new customers that they are not only "virtual assistants" but that they play a vital role in supporting the company – through Crowdsourced Innovation – to better understand its customers and to develop products that better relate to the needs and desires of the users.

Checklist for Crowdsourced Innovation

The "Crowdsourced Innovation Checklist" below summarizes insights gained at innosabi and assists companies in planning effective strategies. This list contains the key questions concerning every step of the process – from the broad, strategic intent to the application of the final result and even beyond its market launch. Answering these questions will provide a structure and offers guidance for the successful implementation of innovative Crowdsourcing projects.

- Meaningful Crowdsourced Innovation projects need to be EMBEDDED IN THE OVERALL CORPORATE STRATEGY (e.g. marketing or innovation strategy). Nevertheless a Crowdsourcing project requires a goal of its own which will vary depending on the focus of the project. Key questions can be: "Do you want to create a new product, discover hidden customer needs or increase brand recognition?". Defining the objective of a Crowdsourcing project is the first important decision to make.

- CHOOSE A TECHNOLOGY for Crowdsourced Innovation, which integrates best practice processes and has been proven in successful reference projects. It should be intuitive to use for the participants and facilitate your collaborative innovation approach with efficient processes.
- Evaluate the viability of a CONFIGURATOR.
- The success of a Crowdsourced Innovation project depends on the TIMELY INVOLVEMENT OF THE APPROPRIATE PARTICIPANTS. Companies must decide which type of participants they want to attract for their project and which backgrounds or expertise the recruited co-developers and idea generators should have.
- Companies should APPOINT A PROJECT AND A COMMUNITY MANAGER to monitor the management of the Crowdsourcing community. This manager is responsible for motivating the community and ensuring continuous engagement.
- Plan a FAIR REWARD STRUCTURE for the participants that takes their motivation into account.
- Developing an APPROPRIATE AND EFFICIENT DECISION MAKING PROCESS is very important. The best method is one that allows an easy flow of creative ideas, but simultaneously

helps to filter out the best ideas in a non-intrusive and controlled way.

- SET UP A LONG-TERM PLAN FOR MAINTAINING THE NEWLY ESTABLISHED RELATIONSHIP with the participants so that the community does not disintegrate and can be activated again in future projects.

Claus Schuh

Social Media Coordinator (2012) at Ford Germany

»We involved end-users in the development of new interior design concepts for our cars. This project went beyond a simple idea contest or open call for suggestions. By starting a dialogue with the participants and helping them to shape out their ideas, we were able to establish collaborative processes with highly valuable results.«

12

TECHNOLOGY FOR CROWDSOURCED INNOVATION

Crowdsourced Innovation is based on the premise that companies are receptive to the multitude of ideas and potential contributors outside their organizational boundaries. These contributors however may be dispersed around the globe, speak different languages, and live in different time zones. Collecting, selecting, and filtering the large amount of information they can provide is a challenge. Even though Crowdsourced Innovation is primarily a social process driven by the involved individuals, its implementation on a large scale is only feasible with the support of technology. This is where Crowdsourced Innovation platforms unfold their potential: they can massively support the interaction of companies with the originators of ideas. Through smart algorithms they support or even automatically identify what ideas are most valuable for an organization. The first step, however, is that customers or end-users begin to share their ideas. This cannot be forced. They have to be motivated to share and their trust has to be earned. We have realized that the functionalities and technical features of our Open Innovation platforms work best, when the platforms themselve embody this culture of trust and sharing. The technology has to reflect and enable the social nature of Crowdsourced Innovation.

Culture of Trust and Sharing

We discovered very early that working with a diverse group of stakeholders needs specific software that is both intuitive for the end-user and efficient for the innovation manager and the associated team. Based on this we defined three core values every Crowdsourced Innovation platform should be built on:

PASSION FOR INNOVATION: The technology should be easy to use and encourage participation via gamification and reward mechanisms. It should spark passion for innovation within all external participants as well as within the company and its key stakeholders – because no innovation project will be successful without passionate individuals driving it.

TIME FOR INNOVATION: Crowdsourced Innovation technology should be designed in such a manner that the users and administrators are able to focus on the truly important tasks. Time should be used for creative ideas, rather than routine tasks and maintenance. The latter should be automated as much as possible. Intelligent functions and algorithms can facilitate moderation and administration, so that time is spent creating innovation and driving promising projects to completion.

OPEN FOR INNOVATION: Crowdsourced Innovation technology should be open for various stakeholders to participate rather than being a closed system. The user base should not be limited and all individuals with relevant expertise, knowledge, or experience should be given the possibility to contribute.

Discover the Best Ideas

The best idea selection processes use the collaborative consensus of the community. This is why the design of your decision-making processes is a key success factor. It should be based on Open Innovation best practices from various industries. When we developed our first Crowdsourcing platform unserAller – today Germany's largest innovation community for consumer goods – we were inspired by design thinking principles and moderated brainstorming techniques. Both drive high engagement with usersand provide a clear decision-making process. The most important aspects are:

ENCOURAGE WILD IDEAS: To encourage the creation of new ideas and out of the box thinking, suggestions should always be posted anonymously. The result of a peer-to-peer voting must be invisible, so that popular ideas are not overemphasized compared to new ideas and people do not mobilize their personal networks to bring their own suggestions to the top.

FOCUS ON RELEVANT CONTENT: Sorting the ideas in a project based on latest entry or highest rating is often the intuitively chosen method, but this can be both discouraging and inefficient. Ideas that are on top of the list remain there simply because they constantly get more attention. Thus filtering mechanisms based on the relevancy of the ideas have to be applied. Intelligent, self-learning algorithms help to channel the community's power and reflect the "interest of the community".

COMBINE THE EFFORTS: Double or similar entries can discourage users and distort evaluation and voting. The technology should therefore encourage both users as well as moderators to combine efforts and group similar ideas. A semantic analysis tool can improve this process and make it more efficient.

Reference Design

We spent several years designing and optimizing our software to solve these challenges. Now we want to share an overview of the required functionalities as a reference design for Crowdsourcing software.

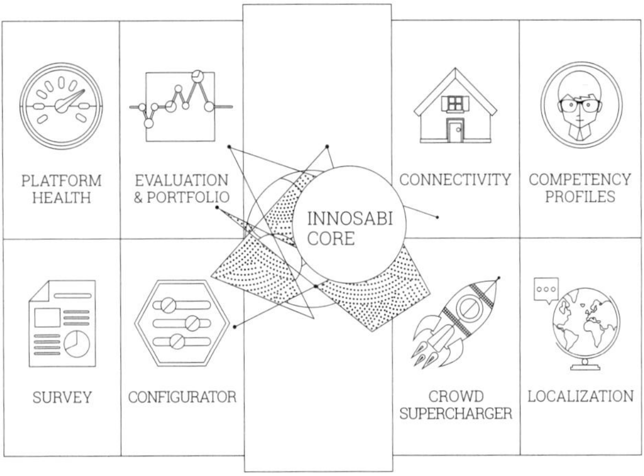

The innosabi technology consists of a core and specific modules, each with a unique function and purpose within the Crowdsourced Innovation process.

These Crowdsourced Innovation principles apply both within the boundaries of a company as well as in connection with customers and external stakeholders. The core functionality – consisting of frontend and backend – is the foundation for any other additional modules.

THE FRONTEND provides the user engine to

- facilitate multiple innovation projects with different types of suggestion formats: e.g. with attachments, rating and tagging, voting mechanisms (peer to peer voting, token voting etc.),

- implement projects with multiple project phases,
- sort suggestions with intelligent algorithms according to the community's interest leading to an unbiased result,
- ensure up to date provision of project information and a feedback channel to the participants with platform and project blogs,
- keep participants informed about actions within their projects,
- collect credits for the quantity and quality of contributions (determined through peer-rating) and visualize the ranked participation in a user leader board.

THE BACKEND ensures the efficient management, allowing

- adjustable degrees of openness for each innovation project,
- moderation interfaces with a functionality to export and classify suggestions,
- identification and merging of similar or duplicate suggestions,
- content management systems,
- automated emails that can be adjusted and customized,
- assignments of user roles and platform rights.

THE PLATFORM HEALTH MODULE supports the management of the community and detects fraud attempts by

- allowing to benchmark our community metrics such as "number of suggestions per participant" or "number of comments per suggestion" with best-practice references based on academic research,
- visualizing benchmark results in the platform backend,
- automating recommendations to improve platform metrics,
- detecting and eliminating fraud.

THE EVALUATION AND PORTFOLIO MODULE enables efficient evaluation of suggestions and facilitates the idea selection process using

- customizable definitions of the evaluation criteria,
- visualizations adding the average evaluation of the community to the evaluation scale, similar to the Delphi method (an interactive forecasting method which relies on a panel of experts, where the opinions of others are shared),
- visualizations of suggestions in a portfolio chart with automatically changing evaluation criteria as x- and y-axis.

THE SURVEY MODULE enhances a Crowdsourced Innovation platform with the possibility to create quantitative surveys, such as

- surveys with standardized question and answer templates, e.g. likert scales, checkboxes, open answers,
- surveys as a selection mechanism for participation in innovation projects,
- surveys as part of multi-phase innovation projects,
- interfaces with competency profiles and
- allowing the export of the survey results via charts and as additional output in excel, csv, or pdf formats.

THE CONFIGURATOR MODULE enables product development through virtual prototyping:

- participants can visualize their suggestions,
- selected suggestions are visible for other users,
- configurator submissions can be moderated,
- the logic flow of the configurator is defined by standardized processes,

- through individual customization of the configurator it is possible to reflect the desired product components and let them be rated by the community.

THE CONNECTIVITY MODULE encourages active, lively, and continuous use of the platform and allows the connection of the projects to social media or widgets on a homepage. It offers

- one-click integration of projects into Facebook via tab applications,
- collection of badges and special statuses for specific knowledge and achievements,
- social sharing functionalities and log-in possibility via the user's Facebook credentials.

THE COMPETENCY PROFILES MODULE gives insights about the community and the individual members. Specific users can be invited to participate in certain innovation projects based on their skill set and experience. Key elements are

- inquiries regarding competencies of participants during the registration process,
- assignment of competencies by the project manager,
- automated assignment of competencies using data regarding participation in pervious projects,
- a detailed filtering mechanism that is based on user competencies allowing targeted invitation to projects.

THE CROWD SUPERCHARGER MODULE enhances an innovation project with direct feedback from around the world in a very short time frame. Elements include

- APIs to the e-collective work communities Amazon Mechanical Turk and Clickworker by Humangrid with an estimated 2 million global participants,
- the possibility to select specific countries and regions,
- fast replies to questions and tasks of your innovation project, e.g. evaluation of ideas or generation of insights.

THE LOCALIZATION MODULE allows implementation and use of the Crowdsourced Innovation platform in multiple languages simultaneously by

- automated translation of user generated content,
- display of translated and original comments via mouse-over,
- translation of platform content (buttons, descriptions, etc.) with our efficient localization interface,
- translation of static pages using our content management system,
- switching the platform language in the user profile settings,
- automated detection of browser language.

The modules and their specific combination not only provide the necessary functionalities for the project, they also set the parameters and boundaries in which the Open Innovation process is embedded. Aligning these parameters and the platform set-up with the goal and desired result of the project is key for its success.

Dr. Stefan Ried

Vice President & Principal Analyst at Forrester Research

»Most buying influence has already shifted from marketing to every consumer's peer base on social networks. The consequent next step in the age of the customer is to empower consumers' influence even further in collaborative innovation. Professionally moderated Crowdsourcing is the most efficient implementation of it.«

13

A UNICORN IS A HORSE DESIGNED BY A CROWD

PROTOTYPES IN CROWDSOURCED INNOVATION

When we think of tangible objects, we usually have a visual representation in mind. Describing these mental pictures with words is very difficult and many aspects or details can get lost in this process of expressing them. Everyone who has ever tried to describe his or her ideal pair of shoes or the perfect apartment furniture to others has experienced this problem. Typically, your descriptions never live up to the great pictures of your imagination and you can never be sure if the person you are talking to actually envisions what you had in mind. This is also a fundamental problem in innovation processes. Without a doubt, many great ideas have been dismissed simply because people were unable to describe them well enough. Therefore, we believe that innovation is a hands-on process. Ideas for innovative products are often too complex to be described in words alone. You have to actually see them, feel them and play with them. That is why we have included prototypes in our Crowdsourced Innovation approach from the early beginning. Now we want to explain how we use such prototypes to enable creativity and improve cooperation within innovation communities.

A Catalyst for Teamwork

One of the strongest benefits of prototypes is that ideas can be evaluated at a very early stage in the development process independently from questions regarding the later implementation. We have experienced that the rougher the prototype, the more room is available for constructive feedback, improvement, and further development. Simply put, raw prototypes are a perfect breeding ground for constructive teamwork. Product development projects that use Crowdsourcing methods often ignore the use of prototypes and only engage in online dialogue. This method is prone to create intangible results that are difficult to translate into implementable solutions. Therefore we have found it to be beneficial – especially for result-oriented Crowdsourcing projects – to use methods that enable either online or offline prototype utilization.

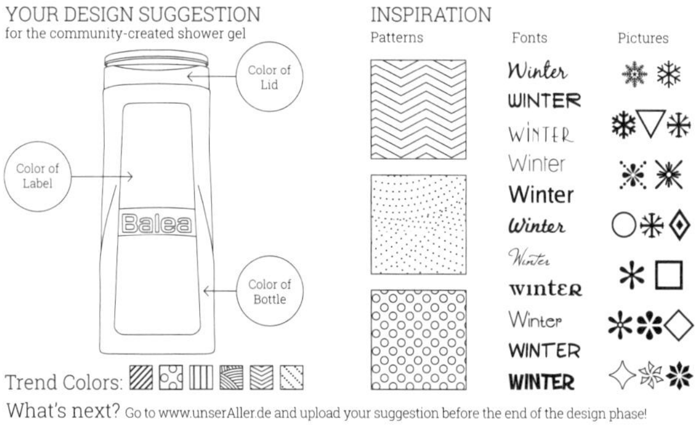

A papercraft set which enables participants to create design suggestions. With the provided colors and elements as inspiration, no professional design expertise is required.

Projects executed via the Crowdsourcing platform unserAller – our engine specifically designed for the consumer goods industry – have shown that the utilization of tactile prototypes leads to better results. At the same time it significantly increases the connection to the brand as well as the active involvement and engagement of the participants. At unserAller we have worked with two different forms of prototype methods: "Papercraft" sets and "Do-It-Yourself" packets.

Papercraft Sets

Papercraft prototypes are models constructed mainly from sheets of heavy paper, paperboard, card stock, or foam. They are suited well for projects with a significant graphic design element like packaging design, fashion, or posters.

They are especially useful for participants who do not have professional design expertise. Participants armed with scissors, glue, colored pencils, or basic knowledge of image editing programs can easily use papercraft prototypes to flesh out their ideas. A papercraft set should contain the following elements:

- Outlines, templates, stencils
- Logos in different sizes, trademark shapes, or images, as well as colors reflecting the company's corporate identity
- Required elements that must be used
- Elements that can inspire and ignite the creativity of the participants (e.g. pictures, shapes, icons, backgrounds, cut-outs, specific fonts, trendy colors)

The papercraft set should be prominently displayed online and easily available for download. Another possibility for easy access is to email the package to registered participants. Printed copies can be sent along with a Do-It-Yourself package, too.

Do-It-Yourself Packets

Apart from the fact that product development is already fun, prototype packages further trigger the enthusiasm of the participants. In many instances, we have observed that they are the main reason for getting engaged in Crowdsourcing projects. They enable participants to visualize ideas, which cannot be adequately explained in words. They also encourage experimentation as well as further development of new ideas and are often the catalyst for completely new ideas.

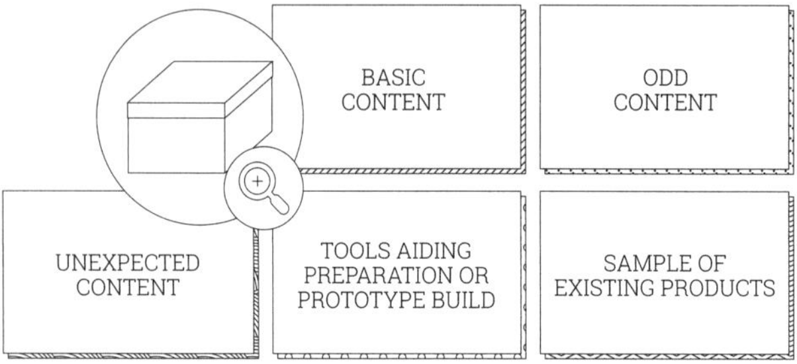

User Innovation Toolkits or prototype packages should contain a variety of different elements to foster creativity and innovative ideas.

The compilation of such packages plays an essential role in presenting and setting the relevant project parameters and at the same time triggering creativity. We recommend to put together such prototype packages – often called "User Innovation Toolkits" – adhering to the following guidelines:

| BASIC CONTENT: Participants should be able to create a basic prototype from the key ingredients contained in the package. This could take the form of a finished product sample where participants can add or change elements and ingredients. The basic content included in the packet guides the participants regarding the creative free space they have to work with. Potential suggestions can either be in a more limited framework

only changing a few specific characteristics or – if the project is aimed towards finding a completely new solution – to come up with completely new ideas.

- ODD CONTENT: Packages should include odd content that by definition fits within the project parameters but may not be the first thing that comes to mind. Such content will eventually lead participants to think about unique solutions and add excitement as well as ingenuity to the process.
- UNEXPECTED CONTENT: Unexpected content includes elements that are a surprise and at first have no relation to the project. This type of content, however, will engage the creativity of the participants and is also a clear sign that other crazy ideas and content not included in the packet are highly welcomed. Of course, this approach is only appropriate for projects with little or no restrictions. Unexpected content should not be included in projects with specific expectations and criteria that should be met.
- TOOLS AIDING PREPARATION OR PROTOTYPE BUILDING: If certain tools make the realization easier or if they are a key prerequisite, it is important to include them in the package. Ideally, these tools should be ready for use and disposable. Otherwise building the prototype can simply fail due to the inability to utilize the adequate resources.
- SAMPLES OF EXISTING PRODUCTS: Samples of existing products that are included in the prototype packages give the participants a feeling for the brand and the product family where

the future product will be positioned. As a nice side effect, the familiarity with existing products increases when samples are included. However, we do not recommend to include samples if the objective of the project is to create a product that should differ significantly from the existing product portfolio.

When including prototype construction in a Crowdsourcing project, companies whose products require specific technical capacities should consider the so-called "maker movement" and "makerspaces", which make use of community owned and shared equipment, facilities and manufacturing tools. Also, locations like TechShop that offer hourly usage of professional equipment and tools are an exciting opportunity technical Crowdsourced Innovation projects can take advantage of.

Operational Details

It is very important to pay attention to the packaging of the prototype parcel. It can be very frustrating to receive damaged content that does not allow the participants to create and submit a prototype or idea in a timely fashion. If something breaks during transit, the organizer of the campaign should be prepared to reimburse the cost incurred by the participant while building a prototype up to a particular limit instead of resending a package that may not arrive on time.

Prototype packages are particularly useful if the discussion of specific topics needs to be encouraged. This also works if a company requires feedback regarding potentially controversial ingredients or parts. If the topic of a food project were "what do you consider to be healthy", the discussion could be further facilitated by asking questions regarding the addition of vitamin C tablets: "Do you consider the addition of vitamins as healthy, unnecessary or even harmful?". Packages can also include different samples to test for optimal usage and/or ranking in order of preference (Another example from the food industry are sweeteners. Packages can include sugar, glucose, honey, artificial sweeteners, dextrose, maple syrup flakes or candy floss to test preferences). The discussion can also be facilitated by packages with different ingredients similar to A/B testing in web design. Asking specific questions, users will rate packages with distinct content – A and B packets – differently.

The decision regarding the number of the sample size to be sent depends on the complexity and cost of the content, shipping fees as well as the number of desired participants. Our experience has shown that a sample size of 20-50 packages is appropriate for projects with a strong focus on innovation, while 500-1,000 units are recommended for projects with the objective of communication.

Finally, it is important to clearly communicate which participants will receive prototype packets. Packages can be sent to the most active participants during the project (determined via a point based reward system), a previously determined group (perhaps an already established customer advisory board), selected bloggers who have a strong follower base, or selected winners of a lottery that took place before the beginning of the Crowdsourced Innovation project. We recommend asking the participants to send back the winning user-designed samples to the company as long as the prototypes are non-perishable and the samples are worth keeping for further development and implementation. To make this happen, participants have to be told early in the process to avoid that they discard their prototypes unintentionally. The return rate for the prototypes will increase if a pre-paid return envelope is included in the original prototype package.

Don't Aim for Final Concepts

When looking at user-generated prototypes, certain company stakeholders often think, "This is unprofessional; our company cannot possibly use this". Thus it is important to have realistic expectations of the users, who are interested in supporting the design of a product but do not necessarily have the competence to translate ideas into marketable products: the latter is the sole responsibility of the company. User-generated prototypes should be viewed as a starting point for a discussion with the participants in the Crowdsourcing project as well as an inspiration and the basis for the product's potential operational execution. Prototypes cannot be one-to-one models for final products.

In sum, creative prototype construction instantly infuses life into your company and your Crowdsourcing project. The true love for the designed products or services, the attention to detail, and the passion for prototype construction that participants show during the project is infectious.

John Bessant

Professor of Innovation & Entrepreneurship at University of Exeter

»With technologies like 3D printing becoming more readily available, users will be able to prototype their ideas in a much more advanced and faster way. This will significantly impact the speed of innovation processes, allowing for quicker iterations and community efforts in prototyping.«

14 CASE STUDY MANHATTAN NAIL POLISH

Sophia Göbel

Product Manager for MANHATTAN at COTY

MANHATTAN is a color cosmetics brand of the global beauty company COTY Inc. sold in several European countries including Germany, where it is one of the top nail polish brands on the mass market. MANHATTAN's core brand values focus on the individuality and personal style of its consumers. The company has a strong history of developing new products in collaboration with external partners such as designers, bloggers, and celebrities. In 2011, MANHATTAN developed a nail polish collection with two fashion bloggers, who documented the entire process on social media. This collection was a success, because end-consumers enjoyed getting behind-the-scenes access and thus felt a close connection with the new collection. As a result of this first success, MANHATTAN embraced the principle of collaborative product development in an even further reaching project: in late 2012, the brand asked its Facebook fans to participate in the creation of a nail polish collection which was named "Community Colours". To make this happen, MANHATTAN launched a project page on the Crowdsourcing intermediary unserAller and integrated the project as a tab application into the brand's Facebook fanpage. The targeted participants included mostly female consumers interested in fashion, beauty, and lifestyle as well as beauty bloggers, who were excited to decide which nail polish colors and designs they wanted to see developed for the next season.

Project Setup

MANHATTAN's key objective was to integrate participants into all aspects and phases of the project. It was important to include as many ideas, wishes, insights, and experiences as possible into the development process in order to receive input for all relevant aspects of the finished product. Therefore, MANHATTAN decided to split its main innovation question – "How should the next season's nail polish line look like?" – into several sub-questions. The project plan consisted of three consecutive phases that built on each other. The sub-questions that drove each phase were:

- PHASE 1: "What theme do you want for your new MANHATTAN nail polish collection?"
- PHASE 2: "What colors should be included in the nail polish collection?"
- PHASE 3: "How should we call the new nail polish colors?"

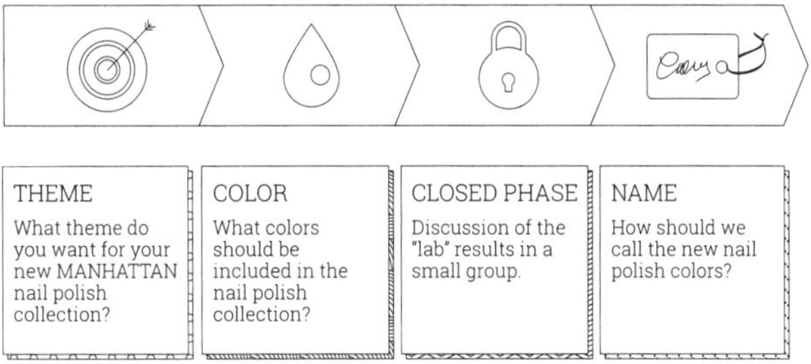

The project was structured in three open phases and a closed discussion, each adressing one specific aspect of the newly created nail polish collection.

During the first phase the participants of the project were invited to submit suggestions as well as mood boards for the general theme of the nail polish collection. The twenty most popular suggestions were put up for a vote, in which the motive "BOHEMIAN LOOK" received the most votes and thus was selected as the guiding theme and name for the collection.

In phase 2, MANHATTAN distributed prototype packages (do-it-yourself or DIY-boxes) to 500 of the most active participants from phase 1 to encourage and support them to bring their ideas to life and to increase their emotional connection to the community-effort. The participants were able to mix the provided color pigments with sparkles, gels and clear nail polish to create prototype nailpolish designs. MANHATTAN provided the outline of their nail polish bottles on design sheets to help the co-creators imagine the newly mixed shades as finished goods, in final packaging and on shelves.

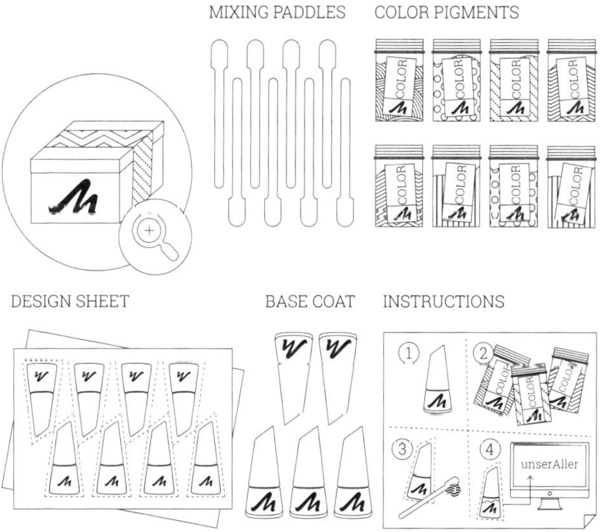

The package provided all necessary ingredients to mix unique nail polish creations as prototypes which were then shared and discussed with the other participants.

Each DIY-box contained the following ingredients:

- A letter summarizing the first project phase and the instructions for mixing the prototypes
- A laminated design sheet with the outline of MANHATTAN nail polish vials for the application and later presentation of the created nail polish colors
- Five bottles of base coat
- Eight color pigments – three primary colors (red, yellow, blue), two non-colors (white, black), glittery pigments (either aluminum, brilliant gold, royal gold), and two additional colors for inspiration (either magenta, ruby red, robin egg blue, hot pink, fawn brown, or opal green)
- Wooden mixing paddles

Even though the prototype boxes were only meant to inspire the co-creators, many participants experimented with other components not included in the box like eye shadow powder or glitters. Some of the color suggestions were submitted with collages that mirrored the particular inspirations for the product as well as the participants' favorite trends and colors. This clearly shows the overwhelming enthusiasm of the crowd to participate; within only two weeks participants submitted over 800 different colors, posted more than 5,000 comments on the project homepage and rated the submissions more than 2,000 times. Ultimately the community voted for twenty colors to be included in the new line.

MANHATTAN was aware that converting a picture or mood board into a pigmented nail polish formula could be difficult. Therefore,

MANHATTAN asked the co-creators of the twenty winning shades to mail in their samples physically and to participate in an exclusive chat. During this step the co-creators worked very closely with company employees to finalize the nail polishes. This exclusive phase presented MANHATTAN with a unique chance to further integrate the winners into the project and to increase their emotional connection with the project and, most importantly, the final product. Furthermore, MANHATTAN was able to ensure that the manufactured nail polishes matched the submissions that thousands of participants helped to create as closely as possible. Thanks to this near to perfect replication, the participants could easily identify the colors they supported and influenced during the development process in the store displays and were eager to buy them.

In the project's third and final phase, MANHATTAN proposed names for each new nail polish shade and users voted for their favorite shade name. MANHATTAN had already selected a list of names and did not allow participants to brainstorm and come up with their own ideas for naming the products, since all the names had to meet copyright requirements. In total, 5,448 votes were cast in this phase.

As an incentive the seventy most active project participants were rewarded with the co-created nail polish line before it was available in stores. However, reactions on social media proved that the main reason most people participated was not to get a free sample of nail polish but to take part in the creative process and to create nail polishes that they envisioned and wanted but could never buy before. By the end of the project, the project website had received over 35,500 visits. Some co-creators spent up to several hours per day on the MANHATTAN project site. The crowdsourced nail polish collection surprised several industry experts, because not a single "classic" red tone was included among the nail polishes, but several shades of green and turquoise. From a Crowdsourced Innovation perspective this is a very logical result: when asked, most customers will not choose options that they can already find on store shelves like traditional red. Instead they will choose options that they crave but cannot find. This provides companies with a great opportunity to identify gaps in the market. Furthermore, crowdsourced products create buzz and attract attention long before they hit the shelves. Engaging a large number of people in Crowdsourced Innovation projects delivers very loyal brand ambassadors who feel engaged in the brand. Apart from this strong customer connection, media attention, especially in social media, was overwhelming. Over 500 blog entries were written about the "Community Colours" nail polish collection long before it was available for sale to the general public.

The Result

The nail polish collection was a sales success as soon as it hit the shelves: it became one of the most successful nail polish displays in MANHATTAN's brand history. The result can be attributed to two main factors: first, MANHATTAN brought a collection of nail polish to the market that catered to its customers' wishes. Second, the collection had hundreds of brand ambassadors creating buzz long before "their" product reached the market.

As MANHATTAN collected great ideas from customers and created a successful new line of nail polish, the company also received additional benefits:

- DISRUPTIVE IDEAS: Participants suggested other ideas beyond pigment suggestions; some ideas challenged the basic idea of using lacquer to apply color to nails.
- MARKET KNOWLEDGE: The participants contributed their distinct knowledge about the beauty market and cosmetic brands. They used this knowledge in discussions to create new and unique products.
- INSIGHTS: During the discussion the co-creators provided deep insights into their usage behavior, e.g. how they use application brushes, how they keep their nail polish ready for use and how they mix existing shades to create new colors. They also offered solutions to various identified problems that were encountered during the design process.

The participants also voiced their desire to continue to co-create with MANHATTAN by discussing their wishes and ideas that went beyond the scope of the "Community Colours" project. MANHATTAN listened and continued to integrate their customers into innovation processes: in 2014 the brand and its co-creators developed the nail polish collection "Birthday Colours" in celebration of the brand's 60th anniversary. This project followed similar principles applied in the "Community Colours" case and the participation rates and the level of collaboration were even higher in the second project.

About COTY Inc.

COTY is a leading global beauty company with net revenues of $4.6 billion for the fiscal year ended June 30, 2014. Founded in Paris in 1904, COTY is a pure play beauty company with a portfolio of well-known fragrances, color cosmetics and skin & body care products sold in over 130 countries and territories. COTY's product offerings include such power brands as adidas, Calvin Klein, Chloé, Davidoff, Marc Jacobs, OPI, philosophy, Playboy, Rimmel and Sally Hansen.

Carsten Knop

Senior Business Editor at Frankfurter Allgemeine Zeitung

»Crowdsourced Innovation projects and the launch of the resulting products are typically accompanied by enthusiastic user generated content. It shows how much consumers value the possibility to become active parts of their favorite brands.«

15

CASE STUDY POSTBANK IDEENLABOR

Sven Siering
Project Manager of eChannels at Deutsche Postbank

Tobias Ehret
Director Online Postbank at Deutsche Postbank

Being a trusted advisor is clearly the key success factor for banks and financial service providers. Due to the recent global economic and financial crisis, the level of confidence in the entire industry, however, has deteriorated substantially. More than ever, customers and investors are demanding an increase in transparency and opportunities to get involved in the banks' decision making processes. To make this happen, banks not only need a stronger customer orientation, but also innovative new products and services. Postbank is pursuing this objective with the creation of a user-oriented innovation process, which uses the target audience as a basis for decision-making and enables their active involvement. The main goal behind this approach is to strengthen the customer relationship and increase customer proximity through engagement in Open Innovation processes. In addition, Postbank pursues the overarching vision to become the most innovative bank in Germany – regarding their products as well as their communication style with the customers. The introduction of a permanent Open Innovation platform is in line with this goal – especially taking into account that currently only 2% of all German banks operate such a platform[31].

Open Innovation Platform

The Postbank Ideenlabor is the pivotal element of this Open Innovation strategy. The online platform is the basis for the new collaborative approach in the bank's customer relationship. The customer is included in the Ideenlabor as an integral part throughout the entire innovation process. Involving customers and interacting with them improves the understanding of customer needs significantly and allows to address them better in the future. In addition, existing and new products or services can be tailored to better fit the profiles and requirements of the customers. The Postbank Ideenlabor is thus paving the way for the bank of tomorrow, which places customers at the center of attention and all its activities.

The Ideenlabor strengthens innovation as an integral part of the corporate culture. It forms an object-oriented framework for the entire process, from initial idea generation to final implementation. For this to work, it is important to ensure the sustainable integration of these processes and their long-term purpose. It must be avoided that the innovation platform is either viewed as a pure "gimmick" for marketing campaigns or yet another channel for feedback or complaints. Instead, this platform puts the customers and their requirements at the center of the bank and its strategy. The acceptance of new products and services by consumers can only be assured, if the collaboration continuously reflects the strategic importance of the customers and their input.

The implementation of the Ideenlabor as a permanent Open Innovation platform is based on a successful pilot project. In 2012 an idea contest was launched to improve the already existing smartphone app "Postbank Financial Wizard" together with the customers. In just seven weeks, more than 30,000 visitors submitted over 500 ideas. Many of the customers' suggestions were developed and implemented as new features in the app, for example the function to track cash expenses. Customer satisfaction was a strong measure for the success of this pilot project: 95% of the participants rated it very good or good. In addition, more than 70% of the participants in the project who were not customers of Postbank considered becoming a customer afterwards. The design and practical implementation of the new Open Innovation platform thus must aim to materialize this potential for the entire company on a long-term basis.

Building a Community

For the long-term success of the Ideenlabor and its integration into the internal processes of the bank, building a relevant community is highly important. The core members of the community – those who are most active and continuously participating – are the backbone of such a platform. Taking into account the complex topics in the financial services industry, the participants have to be chosen carefully. To establish a sustainable backbone, the community of the Postbank Ideenlabor was developed in several stages. This process started with a very small closed group of selected members that was gradually opened up for other existing and potential customers. This core group was recruited from members of the customer advisory board. Since 2006, selected customers contribute in this forum, giving feedback regarding the development of new products and services. Apart from being loyal and active, these participants also have specific knowledge, which is highly relevant for the innovation and development process. In April 2014 the customer advisory board was staffed with new members. In an online campaign, individuals interested in participating could apply. The new formation of the board provided the ideal first user group when launching the Postbank Ideenlabor and built its core community.

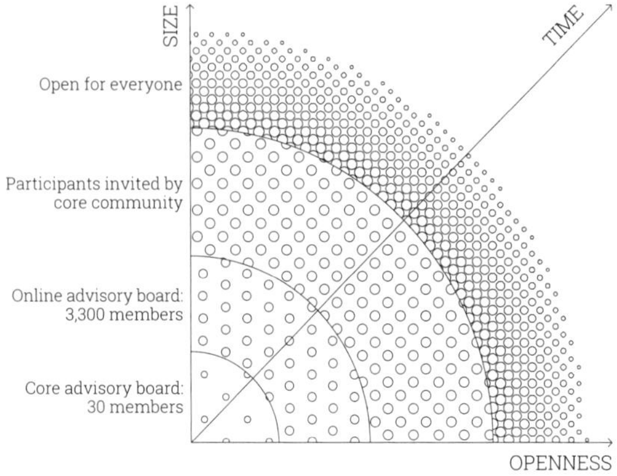

The multi-step strategy for building the community of the Ideenlabor is characterized by a gradual increase in size as well as openness over time.

By gradually opening the platform for different participants, it was possible to control its growth and engage with active members from the very beginning. This of course attracted further participants. When the platform was officially launched, only members of the newly formed customer advisory board were able to participate. Setting this initial restriction was important to incubate a lively and productive discussion that other participants could join easily, once established successfully. In a second phase the extended customer advisory board was able to join. Once part of the community, members can invite more people who will be put on a waiting list until the platform is opened for participants outside the customer advisory board. The opportunity to invite or to recommend other people gives these early members a special position within the community. Furthermore, there is a pre-registration process, in which potential participants can explain their interest and motivation. These participants are penciled in for the next version of the Ideenlabor. The mid-term goal of the Postbank Ideenlabor is to create a forum that has no restrictions regarding participation; inviting all customers and even non-customers to join the discussion.

The Technology of the Platform

The Open Innovation platform was developed in only a few weeks and is based on the technology of innosabi, specifically tailored to the innovation processes of Postbank. Adhering to the defined strategy for building the community, the platform launched with the first user group of 30 representatives of the customer advisory board in July 2014. Soon after, all 3,300 members of the extended customer advisory board were also able to join. Those participants and their composition represent the desired diversity of the community. With an average age of approximately 43 years this advisory board is the youngest in its eight-year history. 25% of the core members are in the age group between 20 to 29 years. Due to their expertise, including younger customers in discussions regarding topics like digitization, mobile services, and smart products is particularly valuable.

The questions asked and discussed on the platform mainly concern the future strategy of Postbank and its offerings. "Are the products of the bank comprehensible and transparent and do those products successfully meet the needs of customers? In which areas can we improve the quality of our services? How can we convince new customers of the benefits of Postbank's services?" No doubt that such questions can be answered best by customers themselves. With its open structure, the platform gives all members of the customer advisory board the opportunity to contribute their own ideas regarding the development or improvement of products and services and to put these suggestions up for discussion in the community. These ideas can be evaluated by other members and can be further developed in a collaborative process.

The initial projects reflect the success of the platform and the positive influence of the carefully structured community. Out of the over 3,000 members 500 to 800 regularly participate in surveys and co-creation projects. Due to the early engagement and invitation to the platform, the participants feel honored being able to contribute in the decision-making processes of the bank: "I am confident that we can really make a difference in the customer advisory board", as one member of the advisory board summarizes the opinion of her and her colleagues. This understanding plays a major role on the platform in order to maintain and strengthen the intrinsic motivation of the participants.

However, the importance of the Open Innovation Platform extends even beyond the involvement of the customer advisory board: It is the starting point for an active and open customer community that is integrated into the banks development processes at all levels. The potential of the Ideenlabor for the strategic direction of the bank has also been recognized at the executive level: "Strengthening the brand of Postbank in an increasingly tough competitive environment is an important topic for the future. Regarding these trends, feedback from the customer advisory board is highly valued. Ultimately, a company like Postbank can only succeed if it is closely aligned with the needs of its customers.", states Hans-Peter Schmid, member of the board and responsible for Branch Sales as well as patron of the customer advisory board.

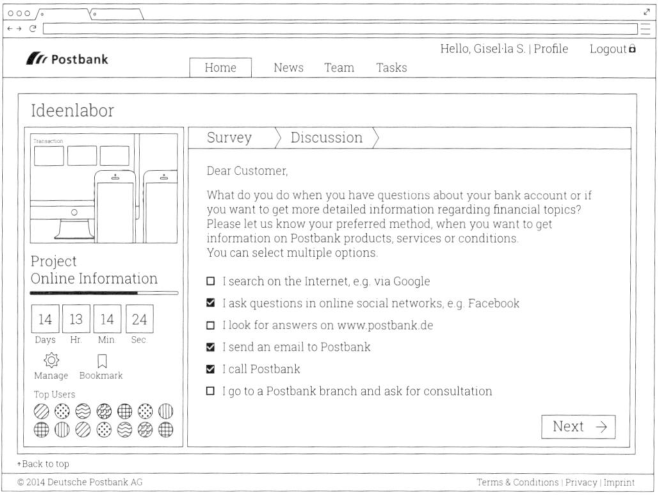

The platform technology of the Postbank Ideenlabor integrates customers into the innovation process with surveys, open idea submission, and discussions.

The launch of the Open Innovation initiative of Postbank has become a success due to two key factors: first, the step-by-step development of the community created a stable core group of participants for the platform. Second, selecting the customer advisory board as the core of this community ensured strong support and acceptance for the project within the entire company. As a highly regarded and well-respected element in the company, it sets the foundation for the

Ideenlabor to become an integral part across all divisions of the bank. In the future, the platform will continue to expand and will become accessible for more user groups and experts, further pursuing the goal of establishing a single, overarching Open Innovation platform for the entire corporation and the needs of the various departments. As such, the Ideenlabor can take the relationship of the bank with its external stakeholders and the quality of its products and services to the next level.

About Deutsche Postbank AG

With around 14 million clients, 14,900 employees and total assets amounting to €158 billion, the Postbank Group is one of Germany's largest financial service providers. It focuses on business with private customers and with small and medium-sized companies. At its own 1,100 branches, it offers extensive financial services as well as postal services. In addition, there are over 4,500 Deutsche Post partner branches where selected Postbank financial services are available, as well as 700 Postbank Finanzberatung advisory centers. 3,000 mobile advisors support Postbank's customers, particularly with mortgage lending and retirement provisions. In online and telephone banking, Postbank boasts a leading position in Germany. The Postbank brand stands for simple, low-cost and fair products for daily use and displays outstanding accessibility across all channels. Deutsche Bank holds 93,7% shares of Deutsche Postbank AG.

Thomas F. Dapp

Senior Economist at Deutsche Bank Research

»In future, the philosophy of Open Innovation is likely to be reflected in many sectors. The use of web and technology-based instruments offers considerable potential for expansion and experimentation. Technological advances will further modernise existing infrastructures; people's digital competence will grow; and new forms of participation and collaboration will emerge. Especially in service driven industries like banking and finance, users and providers will reach a new level of collaboration.«

16

CASE STUDY
ISPO OPEN INNOVATION

Dr. Nina Schniering

Head of Corporate Development at Messe München International

Even in an increasingly connected digital world, brick and mortar trade fairs still offer valuable platforms for communication and exchange: they are important live meeting points for exhibitors and their stakeholders as well as the presentation of novel products, services, and innovative developments. However the status quo and business model of trade fairs and their organizers is challenged: for one, it becomes increasingly harder to meet and engage with trade fair visitors and stakeholders dispersed all over the globe. Why should a customer go visit an exhibitor at a trade show, if they can have face-to-face meetings and browse product and service offerings online? On top of that trade fairs are often events happening once or twice a year, only allowing sporadic exchange. Trade fair exhibitors are questioning the return they can expect from their square meter presence at a trade show, no matter whether this is measured in sales opportunities or leads with potential customers, suppliers, or partners. Relying on selling exhibition space by the square meter alone will no longer be a viable business model for most trade fair organizers. Messe München International (MMI) responds to this challenge by adapting its business model towards becoming a 365 days a year service provider including a broad online services portfolio. This expansion does not render the traditional services irrelevant, the contrary is the case: trade fairs can leverage their existing relationships with exhibitors and visitors. Their position and expertise in certain industries is the foundation for offering unparalleled services by integrating end-users and consumers into the value chain of the existing B2B business model.

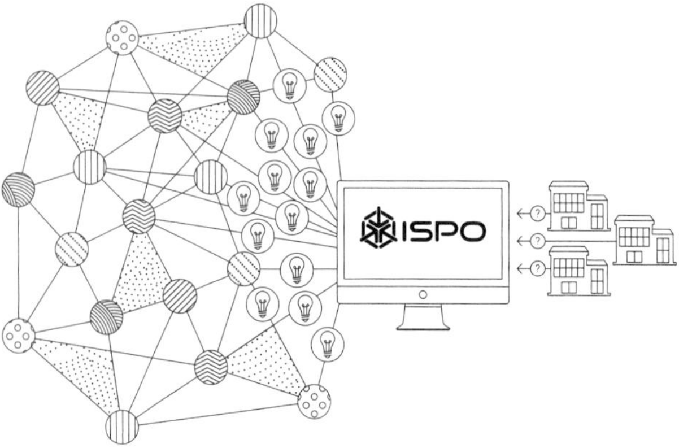

With the Open Innovation platform, ISPO becomes a hub for connecting exhibitors and visitors, not only during the trade fair but throughout the entire year.

A New, Digital Business Model

MMI has expanded its business model along the digital transformation by embracing the opportunities of Crowdsourced Innovation. For ISPO, the worldwide leading trade fair for the sports industry, MMI introduced the ISPO OPEN INNOVATION platform. ISPO's exhibitors and sports industry manufacturers have the opportunity to collaborate with athletes and sports fans from all over the world. In co-creation projects, innovative products and services can be developed. Product testing projects offer manufacturers the opportunity to have prototypes of products or services tested before releasing them to the market. ISPO is a well-established and highly recognized trade-fair in the sports industry with strong ties to manufacturers, sports experts, and retailers from all over the world. These connections are a very valuable asset and constitute the basis for the platform's success. The ISPO OPEN INNOVATION platform connects manufacturers with consumers and end-users to provide an environment for collaborative product or service development and testing. With this platform in place, MMI can extend its conventional B2B model. Instead of providing trade fair services primarily for producers and retailiers, end-users are directly integrated into the value chain. This expansion positions ISPO and MMI as the central hub in its newly created B2B2C business model.

The ISPO OPEN INNOVATION platform is part of the overarching ISPO COMMUNITY, consisting of athletes, ISPO visitors, and sports fans. The community provides a virtual space for discussions and polls about sports-related topics and offers a great pool of potential Open Innovation participants. But the pool of potential participants for Open Innovation projects goes beyond the ISPO COMMUNITY. Companies looking to run a project on ISPO OPEN INNOVATION can address MMI's network of circa 2 million contacts consisting of trade fair exhibitors, visitors, manufacturers, retailers, bloggers, and many other experts from various industries. Many visitors of trade fairs are active sports fans, following their outdoor and athletic passion whenever they can. Many of them also hold jobs in other industries as diverse as chemicals, agriculture, or the automotive industry and also visit corresponding trade fairs. These are the ideal candidates to target for an Open Innovation project as they have knowledge from a variety of industries and experiences reaching beyond the world of sports.

Co-Creating Sports Products

The platform provides several advantages and opportunities for companies – from collecting insights, to product development and prototype testing up to marketing campaigns. By accessing the ideas and feedback of sports experts before the market launch, product development takes into account end-user feedback at an early stage and therefore can better fulfill consumer needs. Manufacturers can use this as a valuable sales argument when presenting their collection to retailers. Since the product was developed collaboratively with end-users, they are more than likely to purchase "their product" and recommending it to their peers and friends, making the product a success on the market. Furthermore, the platform allows international brands to address specific countries or regions with their innovation challenges and gather local input.

The sports industry provides an ideal playing field for a Crowdsourced Innovation strategy. Sports experts naturally carry great enthusiasm and passion for their sport and often feel strong attachment to products and brands they use. Furthermore, athletes often already possess great suggestions how to improve existing products or come up with ideas for entirely new ones. The industry itself is also characterized by an open and direct communication at eye-level. Sports fans are typically highly motivated to exchange information and share experiences with like-minded people. Crowdsourced Innovation can leverage this and create mutual value through connecting manufacturers, retailers, and sports experts.

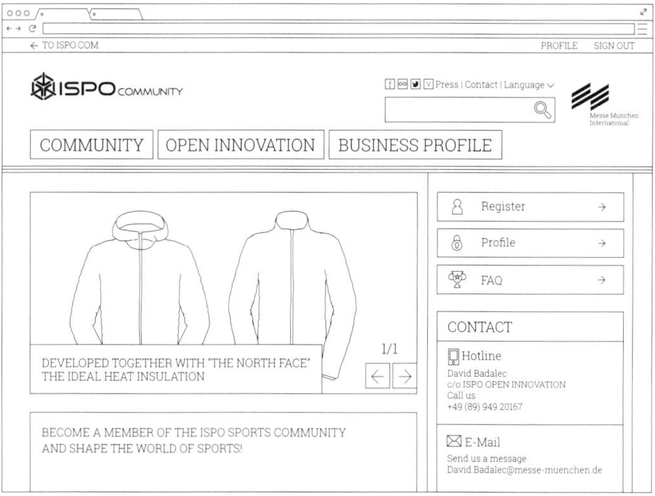

The Open Innovation platform enables producers to reach athletes and sports experts with unique backgrounds and ideas through the ISPO COMMUNITY.

With trade fairs only happening once or twice a year, the Open Innovation platform has started a new era. With the platform, ISPO can provide services the entire year, which is especially important in the sports industry with its large seasonal variety. This service will not replace MMI's core activity as a trade fair organization or its business model. Instead, new possibilities and formats can emerge from combining the existing with the novel approach. ISPO will continue to host trade fairs annually. In combination with the innovation platform, these offline events provide a great possibility to present the results from the platform and develop them even further with visitors, giving the entire fair a new interactive dimension.

Successful Pilot Projects

Since its launch, several successful projects were launched and executed on the ISPO OPEN INNOVATION platform, including cooperations with The North Face, SportScheck, KJUS, and Toray. The North Face invited customers and outdoor athletes to discuss ideas for the development of an adaptable heat insulation technology for outdoor jackets. Arne Arens, General Manager EMEA at The North Face is convinced of the project's success: "The key factor for us was that this platform is independent and has a high reach in our industry and beyond. It brings together the right participants on neutral ground". Also Nico Serena, Member of the Board of Management at KJUS was satisfied with the results of their Crowdsourced Innovation project: "We view the ISPO OPEN INNOVATION platform as an excellent opportunity to gain valuable insights into constantly adapting skier needs as well as a tool to speed up the response time to new innovation ideas".

About Messe München International

With around 40 trade fairs for industrial goods, consumer goods and new technologies, Messe München International is one of the world's leading trade fair companies. Currently, they organize 14 international leading trade fairs, including the largest trade fair in the world, the bauma. Internationally, they organize numerous trade fairs in Asia, Russia, South America, and the Middle East. Each year, more than 30,000 exhibitors and over two million visitors from around the world use their events as industry-specific and targeted communication forums.

Oliver Lang

Vice President Product EMEA at The North Face

»innosabi's platform allows us to harness the ideas of our consumers. Combining the experiences from them wearing our products with our vast knowledge of Product Development creates great synergies to add value to our consumers' needs.«

17

THE CROWD WITHIN

CROWDSOURCED INNOVATION INSIDE COMPANIES

From an outside perspective, innovation and idea management within a company seems like one of the most exciting jobs possible – determining the future of a company by analyzing trends and anticipating market developments. The reality we have faced over the past years, however, is mostly disenchanting. We argue for change in internal idea management, using the methods of Crowdsourced Innovation.

The Suggestion Box

Employee suggestion systems (often still in the form of an conventional letter box) tend to be platforms where employees are submitting ideas to get extra cash rather than generating innovative ideas and creative concepts. Especially short tenured employees such as interns and university graduates often use these systems to improve their salary. Managers or senior leaders, however, do not consider these ideas due to the limited experience of their originators.

Even worse, the employee suggestion box is quite frequently used as a means to express complaints rather than to submit innovative ideas and creative solutions. These systems typically require the employee to submit a suggestion or idea to a direct superior or a dedicated team that evaluates it initially before redirecting it to a relevant division in the company. After a positive second evaluation, the employee who first posted the suggestion is rewarded with a monetary incentive or non-cash prizes like free coffee machines or other consumer products. The level of the incentive also depends on the evaluation of a senior manager and includes elements such as potential company savings or the degree to which an idea can be implemented.

This kind of system is often very time consuming for all parties involved and is perceived as just another annoying task – especially the people evaluating the ideas feel pressured to cast decisions on topics that do not always fall in their field of expertise. In sum, these systems fail to trigger creativity or ideas in a forward thinking manner, as they mostly focus on incrementally improving already existing products or systems.

From Suggestion to Innovation

As a consequence, many companies have established more sophisticated innovation processes to solve the aforementioned problems, tackle trends proactively, and develop new business opportunities. Innovation teams are aiming to create disruptive new offerings and business models. They often start by analyzing market and industry trends and by identifying niches for new offerings. After assembling such an initial framework, they conduct innovation and idea workshops to evaluate early ideas and to allocate development budgets for these projects. However, critical stakeholders or employees outside the innovation team – let alone external users and customers – are often not included in this process until the idea is ready to be tested before the launch.

Crowdsourced Innovation with Employees

The described innovation processes limit many companies, especially those with large workforces. They miss out on a major source for innovation: the crowd from within. Many employees want to be included and want to help shape their company, they want their suggestions and ideas to be heard and they want to be taken seriously. Businesses should crowdsource within their own walls.

Internal Crowdsourcing, however, can only be successful in an environment where employees are consistently encouraged to come up with innovative ideas and are part of the innovation process. The most important characteristic of such a system is true collaboration: posted suggestions and ideas have to be made transparent and visible to all employees allowing them to comment and vote – independent of an employee's role or level of responsibility.

Furthermore, the innovation team should not only ask for general ideas and suggestions, but also propose real innovation challenges, which can be solved collaboratively. Those can be formed into a Stage Gate process with all stages being open to the employees for discussion. In this context, it is recommended to actively display the prevailing thought processes and the current state of research in order to set a transparent and fair "playground" for all participants. Doing so proves that the process is important for the company and that employee input is absolutely relevant for the future of the business. One way to share this information is by integrating an innovation blog into the internal Crowdsourced Innovation system.

Suggestions and ideas should be displayed anonymously so that a participant's title or seniority does not influence how his or her contributions are discussed, improved, or evaluated. Employees are likely to post more daring ideas knowing that their identity or status in the company is not relevant in the corresponding discussion. Comments on original posts, however, should be attributed to a person to ensure a professional conversational tone. Abhi Ingle, Vice President of Ecosystem and Innovation at AT&T, explains why his company's internal Crowdsourcing system has been so successful: "This is a program that gets people excited. Normally, front-line employees could never get an audience with executive leadership, but with the innovation pipeline it's a regular occurrence."[32]

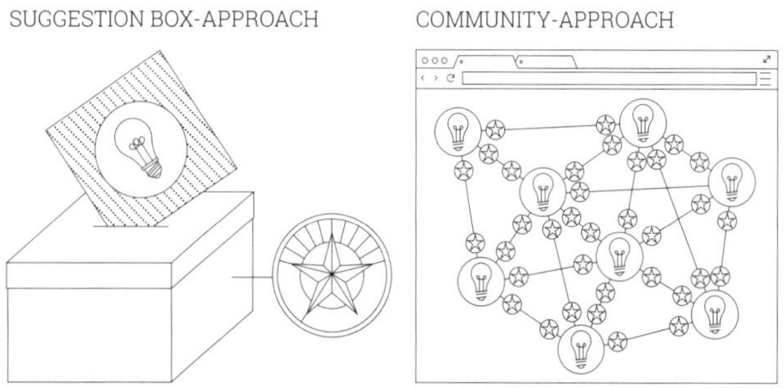

In contrast to accepting or rejecting ideas on the grounds of authority, a community approach is based on a flat hierarchy and the collaborative development of ideas.

Being open to all employees is not only an important criterion for comment boards, it is also true for the evaluation process. It is key that ideas are judged through a true peer-to-peer voting system. Once the crowd has recognized an idea worth pursuing, it can still be assessed via a jury based system that uses specific evaluation criteria like development costs or strategic fit. In order to remove the pressure of making individual decisions – sometimes outside the evaluator's expertise – only ideas pre-evaluated by the crowd will be included in such a system. The evaluations and ratings can be displayed in an automated portfolio that considers both the input of the crowd as well as the one of the jury to support the decision making process.

Finally, gamification elements and re-engagement mechanisms are key in maintaining a vibrant and lively community that returns to the platform regularly to contribute specific knowledge. Gamification can be achieved through a point system or game-like elements, while maintaining an adequate level of professionalism. Re-engagement mechanisms are usually based on social reinforcement, e.g. notifications that alert employees regarding their colleagues' activities and call for support.

In a nutshell, internal Crowdsourcing systems should take the form of communities that tackle innovation questionstogether rather than physical or virtual boxes collecting frustration and criticism.

To take internal Crowdsourcing to the next level, elements of the internal innovation communities need to be combined with external innovation efforts that engage customers and users. Even though it is widely accepted that innovation projects require input from various sources, the information from these sources is not always directed to a single platform where it all comes together. State-of-the-art Crowdsourced Innovation platforms allow this to happen by offering individual settings of complex roles and visibility. Project planners can integrate external and internal stakeholders to varying degrees within the innovation process, thereby turning it into a truly open and collaborative effort, but at the same time establishing a secure and compliant platform.

Case Study: Best Practice Sharing at IABG

The Industrieanlagen-Betriebsgesellschaft (IABG) is one of the leading companies in Europe for industry analysis and testing services. IABG serves customers in the business segments automotive, infocom, mobility, energy & environment, aerospace and defense & security.

Within the defense & security division IABG uses a collaborative approach to share best practices. The innovation community tool connects IABG employees to discuss innovative ideas, client needs and suggestions for new services and customer benefits. Specifically, in a first step painpoints of the customers are defined and discussed. This serves as a starting point to generate ideas for innovative product and service concepts that solve these issues. Ideas are continuously discussed and developed further in the community of employees, who come from various departments and levels of hierarchy.

When IABG implemented this platform, it was of utmost importance to involve a large group of employees in a holistic innovation process – starting with identifying user needs, continuing with creative idea generation processes, and resulting in the selection of the most promising suggestions. Ultimately, these ideas are translated into product and service concepts that can be implemented.

Thomas Sonnenmoser

Vice President Service Defense and Security at IABG

»Our complex offerings often act as a roadblock when identifying the potential for innovative solutions. Drawing the line between an individual offering for one client and the potential for a new, standardized service is difficult. Using an internal community platform, where our employees can discuss our customers' individual pain points and potential solutions enables us to gain a better understanding of our clients' requirements and helps us to develop innovative and sustainable services.«

18

OUTLOOK

CROWDSOURCED INNOVATION – QUO VADIS?

Companies are no longer limited to advertising, marketing, or market research in their interaction with consumers. It is no longer a privilege for small businesses to be the only companies that can have a daily exchange of ideas with their customers. The reality today reflects what the writers of the visionary and iconoclastic Cluetrain Manifesto envisioned fifteen years ago: the marketplace has become a world-wide conversation[33]. In 1999, the Cluetrain Manifesto put forward ideas about the revolutionizing impact the internet would have on markets and organizations. Its most important statement reads as follows:

"A POWERFUL GLOBAL CONVERSATION HAS BEGUN. THROUGH THE INTERNET, PEOPLE ARE DISCOVERING AND INVENTING NEW WAYS TO SHARE RELEVANT KNOWLEDGE WITH BLINDING SPEED. AS A DIRECT RESULT, MARKETS ARE GETTING SMARTER – AND GETTING SMARTER FASTER THAN MOST COMPANIES."

The Cluetrain Manifesto gave business leaders the notion of the internet as a marketplace and helped them to rethink the way they traditionally marketed their products and services. We embed our vision of Crowdsourced Innovation in this context, turning the intangible "target groups" or "demographics" into living and breathing human beings, whose voices need to be heard and whose ideas need to be taken seriously. Companies now realize that they receive major competitive advantages when they reach out to customers, discussing prospects and future offerings with them. We witnessed how companies earn the trust of consumers and yield commercially more successful products and services by opening up their innovation and development processes. The internet enables them to have "human-to-human" conversations, which have the potential to radically transform traditional business practices.

Unfortunately, many companies still fail to tap into the full power of the internet when they use it with a mass-media mind set. Advertising over the web is often seen as the holy grail of online marketing. But this approach does not take into account the true nature of online conversations and customer expectations. Even when companies do decide to open up, many expect the consumer to come to them and are then disappointed by low rates of interaction. What these companies do not yet understand is that they have to work to earn the trust of their customers before any real dialogue can take place.

Earning trust does not happen overnight, once achieved it is not granted forever and can be lost overnight. We see Crowdsourced Innovation as an important building block for constant feedback from customers and other interested stakeholders. But companies must adopt long-term, sustainable Crowdsourcing strategies to accelerate innovation and insight generation if they are to keep up with the changing behaviors and needs of consumers. The biggest appeal of Crowdsourcing is its ability to engage the mostly passive consumers and customers in a company's creative process, turning them into (inter-)active communities and brand advocates. Companies should also integrate Crowdsourced Innovation internally to tap into latent innovation potential and foster innovation through bottom-up contributions from their own employees resulting in increased motivation, engagement and loyalty. Engaging internal and external stakeholders in a fair and transparent way will create a new business culture, ultimately allowing true collaboration.

Fueling Crowdsourced Innovation with Big Data

The questions we are asking ourselves are "Where are we going next?" and "What will be the next big development in Crowdsourced Innovation?". The answers to both of these questions lie in the evolving ways society interacts with and responds to technology. Tools embedded in software and technical devices detect information and collect data, analyzing where we are, what we want and who we are; data is generated every time we use the devices. Technology tracks our every move, web searches, health data such as blood pressure, and where we travel. Sometimes it follows us conspicuously in order to provide certain services like GPS navigation or optimized internet searches, and sometimes it tracks our movements inconspicuously to analyze our behavior to improve the business of others – all the loyalty programs in supermarkets are a prime example. We expect that the next big wave of crowd innovation will stem from these large amounts of data – so called "Big Data" – and the intelligent analysis thereof. But to truly understand the potential of Big Data, the Cluetrain Manifesto again provides valuable insights. When David "Doc" Searls, one of the manifesto's authors, discussed the impact of Big Data with Forbes Magazine in 2013[34], he used the principles from 1999 to highlight the influence of the people who generate the data: "All the talk about 'Big Data' and 'the cloud' is in the B2B space: companies selling services to companies. Individual people are nowhere to be found, except as a source of data, and then mostly through surveillance rather than through conscious and voluntary sharing. At the end of the day, which I think will be a year or two from now, asking what people can do with data will be like asking what people can do with computers or what they can do with networks." We share his vision that data needs to be put in the hands of the people and this is where the innovative power will be in the future.

Data generated by and for users will help them understand themselves better than ever before, and we foresee that this increased knowledge will eventually inspire never-before-seen User Innovation. By connecting self-generated data with our personal feelings, experiences, and needs, we will be able to solve our problems in unique ways. In essence, we will utilize Big Data by individualizing it.

An obvious application will be in the health care sector. Often and sometimes even unintentionally, users generate data on their exercise or diet. With the right analysis of this data and other information, the individual will learn how certain lifestyles and habits affect his or her overall health. The individualization of Big Data will also lead to more user entrepreneurs, since the internet has decreased the start-up barriers for new companies. Some established companies might interpret this development as a threat: new and agile competitors that have very customer-centric views will enter their markets. But this development will also provide new opportunities for companies to build platforms and APIs to which users can connect personally developed devices, solutions, and services. The companies who recognize and utilize User Innovators as a source for corporate innovation will quickly and successfully gain a competitive advantage as long as they offer fair partnerships and fair conditions for collaboration. Therefore, it is vital that protecting and accessing personal data becomes as simple as collecting it, so that it can be available for User Innovation and become a source for Crowdsourced Innovation in companies.

Personal Fabrication and User Innovation

But we do not see Big Data as the only fuel for Crowdsourced Innovation approaches. The personal fabrication trend will take this method to yet another level: when anyone of us, every household, could become a producer or manufacturer; the potential for collaborative innovation becomes infinite.

Personal fabrication breaks through the boundaries between the digital and physical world. Often, it is enabled by 3D printing techniques. With the advancement of such technologies, manufacturing and the structure of production costs will be significantly altered. The effort of producing a single individiualized item is massively reduced and modifications to the product come at negligible cost; only the command code has to be changed. Thus, in the long run, standardization will no longer be the only viable option for large scale production. This corresponds to the reality of the market: consumers want products that are tailored to their individual needs. Competitive advantage for companies lies in the ability to produce goods for a market that is as small as one single person. Thanks to 3D printing, we have the ability to customize objects that are more creative than the ones found in the mainstream market.

The impact on Crowdsourced Innovation is obvious: users will increasingly be able to innovate on their own, relying on factory produced items mainly for standardized products and components. We as consumers will not only print company-designed objects and items, but we will be designing new ones, adapting existing concepts to our personal needs. We will be able to quickly prototype our ideas and build our own products and solutions.

We are urging companies to think about the impact of these developments on their own innovation efforts and how they can engage in these creative environments instead of considering them a threat for their own business model. Companies have to think of personalized fabrication as an innovation technology, that enables the collective development of intangible specifications for tangible products, services, and solutions. Utilizing the potential of personal fabrication is not only limited to engaging external stakeholders; also internal processes can be successfully reshaped.

Fusing Crowdsourced Innovation and Crowdfunding

Lastly, the development of new products and services needs to be financed – in corporate environments as well as in start-up companies. Companies need to allocate resources to those ideas in their innovation funnel that promise most success at market entry. Traditionally this is determined by market research. However, the concept of crowdfunding has opened up completely new ways of funding. An innovative project no longer needs to find a single investor for its realization, but can start convincing future customers to get involved already at the early stages of its development.

This principle is also relevant for corporate innovation processes since it will enable companies to develop products and solutions, which they might have neglected before. Combining Crowdsourced Innovation with crowdfunding leads to an externally dominated innovation process: companies contribute their development resources, their market power, IP, and know-how as well as funding – but all of these elements are open to the enrichment of external stakeholders, who in turn bring the same to the table. In collaboration, these efforts will be able to bring new products and services to market much quicker and with a higher probability of success. Of course, such a model can only succeed when carefully crafted in a way that is fair to all parties and pays tribute to the individual's contribution.

First applications of this approach can alredy be found in many software companies: clients who request new features often contribute upfront to the development with a partial payment, instead of purchasing an individualized programming service. This way, they allow the software company to sell the feature to other customers after a period of exclusivity. Based on their needs, the clients are usually the ones who come up with the idea for new features in the first place.

The Vision: Companies as Networks and Enablers of Innovation

The long-term perspective that we are describing aims at a truly networked company: corporations that create value by connecting, not solely by producing. Companies will increasingly find themselves to be hubs for networks, enabling innovation, rather than being the entities deciding and producing their offerings. Value will be created through connections and networks, as impact does not stem from isolated efforts; it requires collective action and fair collaboration.

Early signs of this development can be found in the past trend of outsourcing, when companies moved their production, their customer service, or even their marketing efforts to contractors. These outsourcing approaches already turned companies into coordinating entities, juggling the many different stakeholders they are working with instead of owning and completing the tasks themselves in isolation. Crowdsourced Innovation takes this development one step further. What if companies truly started acting as trustful networks, providing their network of collaborators with access to corporate assets? What if they became an ecosystem of resources, inspiration, and opportunities for collaboration in order to drive innovation and sustainable value creation?

Start thinking now about what policies and processes need to be in place in order to turn your company into a networked corporation. We see unlimited opportunities for enterprises that are willing to step up. The companies that get it right will find themselves with better insight into their customers, more-innovative products and services, and an increased agility to retool themselves with the skills necessary to respond to the changing technology landscape. We ask you: How are you going to position your enterprise to reap the rewards of Crowdsourced Innovation?

Dr. Kai Grassie

Senior Vice President Corporate Innovation at BSH

Bosch und Siemens Hausgeräte Germany

»The digital transformation is already embedded in the market for home appliances: we are not only thinking about how to manufacture great refrigerators and washing machines, but investing a lot of time to find out how we can better connect our users and devices in order to create value.«

AUTHORS

Catharina van Delden is the co-founder and CEO of innosabi. She holds an MBA from the Technical University of Munich (TUM) and UC Berkeley, majoring in innovation and business creation. In her undergraduate studies, she focused on marketing and life & food sciences. Before founding innosabi, she worked in the marketing department of OSRAM and OSRAM India in Delhi. As a member of the presiding committee of BITKOM, the German industry association of the ITC industry, Catharina represents the interests of start-ups in the digital sector. In 2014, the German Informatics Society honored her with the "digital mind" award for her role as thought leader in Germany's digital development. She was also named one of the 50 most influential women in German IT by the magazine Computerwoche.

David Chia is a Crowdsourcing Analyst at innosabi. He studied communication science and psychology at the Ludwig-Maximilians-University Munich (LMU) and the University of Cincinnati, Ohio. In his Masters studies in Consumer Affairs at the Technical University of Munich (TUM), he specialized in innovation management and consumer behavior research. David received the Germany Scholarship for excellent academic achievement and the Best Thesis Award 2012 of the LMU Department of Communication Science and Media Research for his bachelor thesis. Before joining innosabi, he acquired work experience in marketing, NGO consulting and journalism. Applying his academic background and practical insights gained at innosabi, he contributed several chapters to this book and helped to edit and conceptualize it.

CONTRIBUTORS

Tobias Ehret

is director of Online Postbank, responsible for online and mobile banking. He leads the team that drives Postbank's Open Innovation initiative "Postbank Ideenlabor". Tobias Ehret has been working for Postbank for more than 10 years.

Sophia Göbel

is a product manager for the brand MANHATTAN at COTY Beauty, responsible for product development in the color cosmetics category nail. She studied international business with emphasis on marketing in Germany and the Netherlands. She has several years of international work experience in the beauty industry, including companies such as Beiersdorf, Kalina and COTY.

Alexander Lang

is founder and CEO of IMAN Solutions GmbH, a Munich-based consultancy which focuses mostly on Innovation Management, Change Management and Product Development. Additionally he is employed at the Technical University Munich as research fellow, where he works on projects in the area of Open Innovation and Open Organization. Before, Mr. Lang was Partner at the Siemens Innovation Management Consultancy, where he was responsible for the topics Competency Management and Open Innovation. Till the end of 2008, he was Director Marketing und Innovation at Webasto, a company in the automotive Industry with a turnover of around €2 billion. Prior he worked as a consultant for Ernst & Young and Droege & Comp AG in the areas of Restructuring and Sales and Marketing. Mr. Lang holds a Masters degree in Chemistry of the University of Munich where he graduated in 1997.

Kathrin M. Möslein

is professor of information systems with a focus on innovation and value creation at the University of Erlangen-Nuremberg. She is also a research professor and member of the team of directors at the Center for Leading Innovation & Cooperation (CLIC) at HHL Leipzig Graduate School of Management. In addition, she serves as a member of the advisory boards of the Peter Pribilla Foundation at the Technical University of Munich (TUM), the Cambridge Service Alliance (CSA) at the University of Cambridge and the Fraunhofer IIS-SCS, Erlangen. Amongst others she is a founding member and has been a Vice President of the European Academy of Management (2006-2012). Kathrin has been researching, teaching and consulting in the field of strategic innovation and innovation systems since the early 1990s. Her current research focuses on the implementation of innovation strategies and technologies as well as leadership systems in service organizations.

Andreas Nicklas

is responsible for business development in EMEA at Lithium. Lithium is the market leader for social business solutions built on communities. He is a professional with over 20 years of experience in consulting, sales, marketing, business, and corporate development working for leading international IT companies. Since 2009

Andreas has conducted numerous e-commerce, gamification and social business projects as a consultant, including a social network acting as a member of the managing board. Leveraging his business knowledge Andreas is giving lectures as adjunct professor for studies and executive MBAs at the Technical University of Munich, the University of St. Gallen, Zurich University of Arts and conducted joint research with the University of Zurich. Andreas earned a university degree in Medical Computer Science from the University of Heidelberg.

Frank Riemensperger

born in 1962, studied Computer Science in Germany and the United States and graduated in 1987. Frank joined Accenture in 1989 and specialized in complex IT enabled business transformation programs for large organizations. In 1998, Frank was admitted to the Partnership, which was transformed into the Accenture corporation in 2001. From 1998 to 2005 Frank held various management roles for the Accenture German, Swiss and Austrian geographical unit and was part of the Accenture local management board. From 2002 through 2007, Frank also served as the Deputy Country Managing Director Germany. In 2005 Frank was asked to lead the global Systems and Integration Technology Business of Accenture's largest operating unit "Products". In this role, he was responsible for establishing and expanding IT service centers around the globe, especially in India, the Philippines, Brazil, and China. From 2007 through summer 2009, Frank lived with his family in the U.S., working out of New York, expanding Accenture's Technology Business around the globe. In November 2009, Frank Riemensperger was appointed Geographic Unit Managing Director for Germany, Switzerland and Austria. In this role, he is responsible for Accenture's market development in the German-speaking countries. Currently, Accenture has more than 6,000 employees in this region.

Matias Roskos

is Community Manager at ProSiebenSat.1 Media AG. He is the author of the book "Social media communities" and active as a lecturer in the Social Media Academy. He has been a Crowdsourcing expert since the very beginning of the concept and blogs on the topic at www.socialnetworkstrategien.de.

Nina Schniering

is Head of Corporate Development at Messe München GmbH. She is responsible for the development and operationalization of the corporate strategy as well as the conception of OPEN INNOVATION as a new digital service of Messe München.

Sven Siering

has been working for Deutsche Postbank AG since 2004. He leads a team, which is responsible for innovation and customer service in the e-finance department. Sven holds a degree in business administration from the European University Viadrina and can call on many years of experience in online business.

ACKNOWLEDGEMENTS

Just like the concepts we describe in this book, its creation has been a truly collaborative effort. It has my name on the cover, but was significantly influenced by the entire innosabi team – all methods have been developed by our incredible employees over the years and have been tested in projects with our customers who trusted our innovative approach to innovation. Of course, the main drivers of the methods and practices and our success as a company since 2008 are our founding team, apart from myself JAN FISCHER, MORITZ SEBASTIAN WURFBAUM and HANS-PETER HEID.

When it comes to actually compiling and finalizing this book, major thanks has to go to our fantastic advisory board member BARBARA WITTMANN, who has not only contributed countless hours discussing, conceptualizing, and revising but most of all has motivated us in hours of exhaustion and always believed in us. DAVID CHIA, a lively mind with tremendous writing skills, has co-authored the book and contributed chapters such as "The Power of Users as Innovators" and "The Evolution of Consumer Behavior". Apart from writing we wanted to visualize the most important concepts. With GISEL·LA SAPIÑA FEBRERO and JULIA GACKSTETTER we have two creative geniuses on our team who have made the wonderful appearance of this book possible. Writing a book in a language that is not your native tongue requires excellent editors, and we are so happy to have found them in LANDON REITZ and SEAN BERG.

None of this would have been possible without the unwavering support, encouragement, insights, and patience of my soulmate and husband.

INDEX

R

S

T

U

V

W

SOURCES AND LITERATURE

The Importance of Crowdsourcing

1 Gartner. "*Top Predictions 2014: Plan for a Disruptive, but Constructive Future.*" October 2013. http://www.gartner.com/doc/2602915/

Introduction to Crowdsourced Innovation

2 Howe, Jeff. "The Rise of Crowdsourcing." *WIRED*, 2006. http://wrd.cm/1nkRGsc/

3 Howe, Jeff. *Crowdsourcing: Why the Power of the Crowd is Driving the Future of Business.* New York: Crown Business, 2008.

4 Miller, Peter. "Swarm Theory." *National Geographic*, 2007. http://bit.ly/1DyBtDh/

5 Chesbrough, Henry. *Open Innovation: The New Imperative for Creating and Profiting from Technology.* Boston: Harvard Business School Press, 2003.

The Evolution of Consumer Behavior

6 Trendwatching.com. "*Trend Briefing: Presumers.*" November 2012. http://trendwatching.com/trends/presumers/

7 "Crowd funding campaign The Ocean Cleanup successfully completed." *The Ocean Cleanup*, September 2014. http://bit.ly/1uORoLm/

The Power of User Innovators

8 v. Hippel, Eric (for an overview of his work on User Innovation visit his homepage http://evhippel.mit.edu/)

9 v. Hippel, Eric. "Sticky Information and the Locus of Problem Solving: Implications for Innovation." *Management Science*, 40, 1994: pp 429-39.

10 Ogawa, S. & Pongtanalert, K. *Visualizing Invisible Innovation Continent: Evidence from Global Consumer Innovation Surveys.* Working Paper SSRN, 2011. http://ssrn.com/abstract=1876186/

11 v. Hippel, E., de Jong, J.P. & Flowers, S. "Comparing Business and Household Sector Innovation in Consumer Products: Findings from a Representative Study in the United Kingdom." *Management Science*, 58, 2012: pp 1669–81.

12 ibid.

Branded Communities for Crowdsourced Innovation

13 "Lidl #1 European Food Retailer on Facebook." *Socialbakers.com*, April 2014. http://bit.ly/1eKlGW7/

14 ComBlu. "*The State of Online Branded Communities.*" November 2012. http://bit.ly/1tPrfOY/

15 Nielsen. "*Global Trust in Advertising and Brand Messages.*" September 2013. http://bit.ly/1wF6Avu/

16 Wu, Michael. *The Science of Social 2*. San Francisco: Lithium, 2013.

17 Gartner. "*Gartner predicted that by 2014, 70 percent of proprietary communities would fail.*" 2012.

The Emergence of Platforms

18 Bullinger, A.C. & Moeslein, K.M. "Innovation Contests – Where are we?" *Amcis 2010 Proceedings*, Paper 28, 2010. http://aisel.aisnet.org/amcis2010/28/

19 ibid.

20 "Facts & Stats." *InnoCentive*, October 2014. http://www.innocentive.com/about-innocentive/facts-stats/

21 "OScar - Reinvent Mobility." *The OScar Project*, October 2014. http://www.theoscarproject.org/

22 "A World of Vehicle Innovations". *Local Motors*, October 2014. https://localmotors.com/about/

23 Reichwald, R. & Piller, F. *Interaktive Wertschöpfung - Open Innovation, Individualisierung und neue Formen der Arbeitsteilung*. Wiesbaden: Gabler, 2006.

24 v. Hippel, Eric. *Democratizing innovation*. Cambridge: MIT Press, 2005.

25 Gershenfeld, Neil. *FAB - The Coming Revolution on Your Desktop - From Personal Computers to Personal Fabrication*. Cambridge: Basic Books, 2005.

26 Moeslein, K.M. & Bansemir, B. "Strategic Open Innovation: Basics, Actors, Tools and Tensions." In: Hülsmann, M., and Pfeffermann, N. (Eds.). *Strategies and Communications for Innovations*. Berlin: Springer, 2011: pp 11-23.

27 Moeslein, K.M., Huff, A. & Reichwald, R. "Corporate Open Innovation: Learning from Longitudinal Exploratory Research." *International Journal of Knowledge-Based Organizations*, 2, 2012: pp i-x.

28 Moeslein, Kathrin M. "Open Innovation: Actors, Tools and Tensions." In: Huff, A., Moeslein, K.M., and Reichwald, R. (Eds.). *Leading Open Innovation*. Cambridge: MIT Press, 2013: pp 69-85.

The Crowdsourced Innovation Canvas

29 Osterwalder, A., Pigneur, Y. & Clark, T. *Business Model Generation : a Handbook for Visionaries, Game Changers, and Challengers*. Hoboken, NJ: Wiley, 2010.

Implementing Crowdsourced Innovation

30 "Do Us A Flavour." Cream, 2010. http://bit.ly/1u8XMAk/

Case Study Postbank Ideenlabor

31 IBM & Fraunhofer IAO. "Trendstudie Bank & Zukunft 2014." September 2014. http://ibm.co/1zLiUz4/

Crowdsourced Innovation inside Companies

32 "AT&T's Innovation Pipeline Engages 130,000 Employees." *Forbes*, May 2013. http://onforb.es/1kfB5ji/

Crowdsourced Innovation — Quo Vadis?

33 Levine, R., Searls, D., Weinberger, D. & Locke, C. *The Cluetrain Manifesto: The End of Business as Usual*. Cambridge: Perseus, 1999. http://www.cluetrain.com/

34 "What Can People Do With Data That Companies Can't." *Forbes*, June 2013 http://onforb.es/1tIfhpl/

REFERENCES FOR ILLUSTRATIONS

i Accenture. *"Accenture Technology Vision 2014."* January 2014. http://bit.ly/1gmH0qs/

ii Chesbrough, Henry. *Open Innovation: The New Imperative for Creating and Profiting from Technology.* Boston: Harvard Business School Press, 2003.

iii v. Hippel, E., Ogawa, S. & Jong, J.P.J. "The Age of the Consumer-Innovator." *MIT Sloan Management Review*, 53, 2011: pp 27-35.

iv Wu, Michael. *The Science of Social 2.* San Francisco: Lithium, 2013.

v ibid.

vi Osterwalder, Alexander. "The Business Model Canvas." *Business Model Generation*, 2014. http://businessmodelgeneration.com/canvas/bmc/